I0461509

Compiled by

Frater Lachesis Peyton

Tat Tvam Asi

SAKLAS
PUBLISHING

The Libri of the Probationer

Saklas Publishing, 2026

ISBN 979-8-9943016-3-0

A Note on this Series

The volume you hold is one of a series of companions to the work of the A∴A∴, the spiritual order established by Aleister Crowley and George Cecil Jones in 1907 and governed, in its inner life, by principles far older than either man. Each book in the series gathers into a single binding the official *libri*—the instructional texts—assigned to a particular grade of the Order.

The Probationer volume collects the writings that orient the newcomer and outline the first practices. The Neophyte volume presents the curriculum for those who have entered the Outer College in earnest. The Zelator volume carries the aspirant further, into deeper work with breath, will, memory, and the central scriptures of Thelema. Additional volumes, corresponding to higher grades, may follow in time.

The contents of each volume were determined by cross-referencing three primary sources. The first is Liber CLXXXV, *Liber Collegii Sancti*, the Class D document that sets out the official tasks, examinations, and oaths for every grade from Probationer to Adept. This text specifies which *libri* the aspirant at each grade is required to study, memorize, or master. The second is Liber CCVII, the *Syllabus of the Official Instructions of the* A∴A∴, which catalogues the full corpus of Order publications by class and number, with a description of each. Originally published in *The Equinox* I (10) in 1913 and subsequently revised, it serves as the authoritative index of what each liber is and where it stands in the system.

The third source is James A. Eshelman's *The Mystical and Magical System of the A∴A∴* (College of Thelema, 2000), a modern study that organizes the grade-by-grade curriculum into a practical working format, drawing on all available primary documents—including Liber XIII (*Graduum Montis Abiegni*), *One Star in Sight*, and the 1919 "Præmonstrance" and "Curriculum"—to clarify which texts belong to which grade when the official sources are ambiguous or incomplete. Where these three authorities agree, the assignment is straightforward. Where they differ, editorial judgment has been exercised, and such choices are noted where relevant.

These compilations contain only the *libri* themselves. Each grade of the A∴A∴ also prescribes a broader reading list that may include works by other authors—the *Tao Te Ching*, the *Dhammapada*, Patanjali's *Yoga Sutras*, the writings of David Hume, and others—as well as practices to be carried out under the guidance of a superior. Those external readings are not reproduced here. The present volumes are intended as a practical convenience: a way to keep the core instructional texts of a given grade together, in order, and in a readable form, so that the student may study them without hunting through scattered and sometimes unreliable sources.

The texts themselves carry a classification that the reader should understand.

Class A publications are writings received in a state of illumination, held to be supernally inspired, and not to be altered so much as by the style of a letter.

Class B writings are works of scholarship or informed exposition by individual adepts.

Class C is material suggested by A∴A∴ theory but not official.

Class D publications are the official rituals, instructions, and examination papers of the Order, setting out what is to be done and how.

Class E consists of public manifestos and other broadsheets. Some publications are composite, pertaining to more than one class.

The reader will find texts of several classes within each volume, and should approach them accordingly: a Class A text demands a different quality of attention than a Class D instruction on how to perform a ritual, though both are essential to the work.

THE LIBRI

OF THE

PROBATIONER

⊙

Being the Official Instructions of the A∴A∴

for Those Who Seek Admission

to the Holy Order

V.V.V.V.V.

SAKLAS PUBLISHING

CONTENTS

INTRODUCTION

The texts gathered in this volume constitute the essential curriculum for the grade of Probationer in the A∴A∴, the spiritual order founded by Aleister Crowley and George Cecil Jones in 1907. These instructions have guided aspirants to the Great Work for over a century.

The Probationer's task, as set forth in Liber CLXXXV, is "to obtain a scientific knowledge of the nature and powers of my own being." The texts herein provide the theoretical foundation and practical methods for this sublime undertaking.

The aspirant is advised to read these texts repeatedly, with increasing depth of meditation upon their meaning. Let the Student approach these mysteries with reverence, diligence, and that holy enthusiasm which is the mark of the true Seeker.

Sol in Capricorn

I.

LIBER COLLEGII SANCTI

SUB FIGURÂ CLXXXV

Being the Tasks of the Grades and Their Oaths

Proper to Liber XIII

V

A∴A∴

Publication in Class D

The Task of a Probationer

0. Let any person be received by a Neophyte, the latter being responsible to his Zelator.

1. The period of Probation shall be at least one year.

2. The aspirant to the A∴A∴ shall hear the Lection (Liber LXI) and this note of his office; IF HE WILL, shall then procure the robe of a Probationer; shall choose with deep forethought and intense solemnity a motto.

3. On reception he shall receive the robe, sign the form provided and repeat the oath as appointed, and receive the First Volume of the Book.

4. He shall commit a chapter of Liber LXV to memory; and furthermore, he shall study the Publications of the A∴A∴ in Class B, and apply himself to such practices of Scientific Illuminism as seemeth him good.

5. Beside all this, he shall perform any tasks that the A∴A∴ may see fit to lay upon him. Let him be mindful that the word Probationer is no idle term, but that the Brothers will in many a subtle way prove him, when he knoweth it not.

6. When the sun shall next enter the sign under which he hath been received, his initiation may be granted unto him. He shall keep himself free from all other engagements for one whole week from that date.

7. He may at any moment withdraw from his association with the A∴A∴ simply notifying the Neophyte who introduced him.

8. He shall everywhere proclaim openly his connection with the A∴A∴ and speak of It and Its principles (even so little as he understandeth) for that mystery is the enemy of truth. One month before the completion of his year, he shall deliver a copy of the record to the Neophyte introducing, and repeat to him his chosen chapter of Liber LXV.

9. He shall hold himself chaste, and reverent toward his body, for that the ordeal of initiation is no light one. This is of peculiar importance in the last two months of his Probation.

10. Thus and not otherwise may he attain the great reward, YEA, MAY HE ATTAIN THE GREAT REWARD!

The Oath of a Probationer

I, _____, being of sound mind and body, on this _____ day of _____ [An _____ ☉ in _____ ° of _____] do hereby resolve: in the Presence of _____, a Neophyte of the A∴A∴:

To prosecute the Great Work: which is, to obtain a scientific knowledge of the nature and powers of my own being.

May the A∴A∴ crown the work, lend me of Its wisdom in the work, enable me to understand the work!

Reverence, duty, sympathy, devotion, assiduity, trust do I bring to the A∴A∴ and in one year from this date may I be admitted to the knowledge and conversation of the A∴A∴!

Witness my hand _____

Motto _____

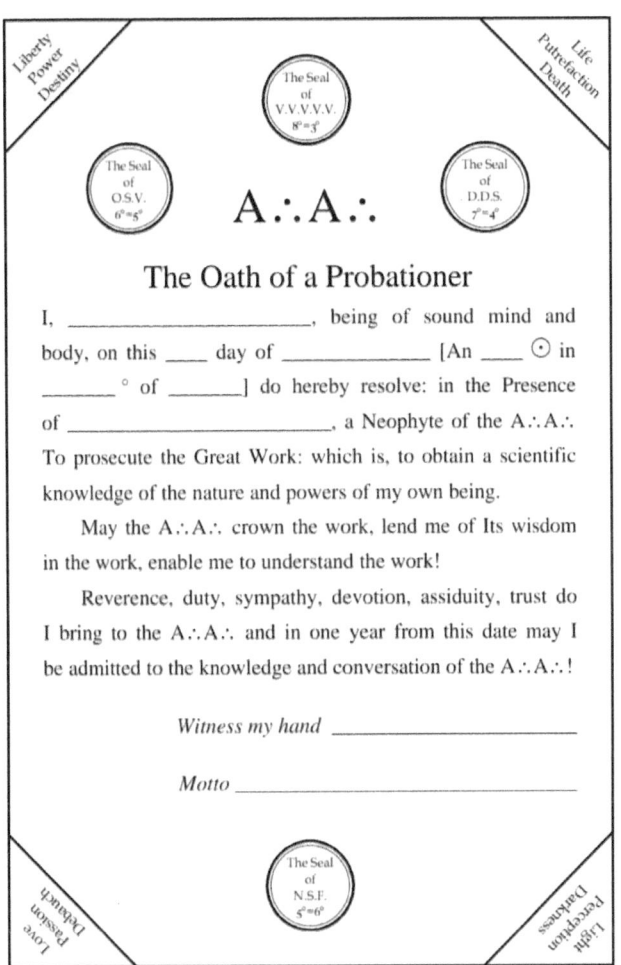

Liberty
Power
Destiny

Life
Putrefaction
Death

The Seal
of
V.V.V.V.V.
8°=3°

The Seal
of
O.S.V.
6°=5°

The Seal
of
D.D.S.
7°=4°

A∴A∴

The Oath of a Probationer

I, _____, being of sound mind and body, on this ____ day of _____ [An ____ ☉ in _____ ° of _____] do hereby resolve: in the Presence of _____, a Neophyte of the A∴A∴ To prosecute the Great Work: which is, to obtain a scientific knowledge of the nature and powers of my own being.

May the A∴A∴ crown the work, lend me of Its wisdom in the work, enable me to understand the work!

Reverence, duty, sympathy, devotion, assiduity, trust do I bring to the A∴A∴ and in one year from this date may I be admitted to the knowledge and conversation of the A∴A∴!

Witness my hand _____

Motto _____

The Seal
of
N.S.F.
5°=6°

Love
Passion
Debauch

Light
Perception
Darkness

The Oath of a Probationer with Seals of the Chiefs

The Task of a Neophyte

0. Let any Probationer who has accomplished his task to the satisfaction of the A∴A∴ be instructed in the proper course of procedure: which is:—Let him read through this note of his office, and sign it, paying the sum of One Guinea for Liber VII which will be given him on his initiation, and One Guinea for this Portfolio of Class D publications, B-G. Let him obtain the robe of a Neophyte, and entrust the same to the care of his Neophyte. He shall choose a new motto with deep forethought and intense solemnity, as expressing the clearer consciousness of his Aspiration which the year's Probation has given him. Let him make an appointment with his Neophyte at the pleasure of the latter for the ceremony of Initiation.

1. The Neophyte shall not proceed to the grade of Zelator in less than eight months; but shall hold himself free for four days for advancement at the end of that period.

2. He shall pass the four tests called the Powers of the Sphinx.

3. He shall apply himself to understand the nature of his Initiation.

4. He shall commit to memory a chapter of Liber VII; and furthermore, he shall study and practice Liber O in all its branches: also he shall begin to study Liber H and some one commonly accepted method of divination. He will further be examined in his power of Journeying in the Spirit Vision.

5. Beside all this, he shall perform any tasks that his Zelator in the name of the A∴A∴ and by its authority may see fit to lay upon him. Let him be mindful that the word Neophyte is no idle term, but that in many a subtle way the new nature will stir within him, when he knoweth it not.

6. When the sun shall next enter the sign 240° to that under which he hath been received, his advancement may be granted unto him. He

shall keep himself free from all other engagements for four whole days from that date.

7. He may at any moment withdraw from his association with the A∴A∴, simply notifying the Zelator who introduced him.

8. He shall everywhere proclaim openly his connection with the A∴A∴ and speak of It and Its principles (even so little as he understandeth) for that mystery is the enemy of truth. Furthermore, he shall construct the magic Pentacle, according to the instruction in Liber A. One month before the completion of his eight months, he shall deliver a copy of his Record to his Zelator, pass the necessary tests, and repeat to him his chosen chapter of Liber VII.

9. He shall in every way fortify his body according to the advice of his Zelator, for that the ordeal of advancement is no light one.

10. Thus and not otherwise may he attain the great reward, YEA, MAY HE ATTAIN THE GREAT REWARD!

The Oath of a Neophyte

I, _____ (old motto), being of sound mind and body, and prepared, on this _____ day of _____ [An _____ ☉ in _____ ° of _____] do hereby resolve: in the Presence of _____, a Zelator of the A∴A∴:

To prosecute the Great Work: which is, to obtain control of the nature and powers of my own being.

Further, I promise to observe zeal in service to the Probationers under me, and to deny myself utterly on their behalf.

May the A∴A∴ crown the work, lend me of Its wisdom in the work, enable me to understand the work!

Reverence, duty, sympathy, devotion, assiduity, trust do I bring to the A∴A∴ and in eight months from this date may I be admitted to the knowledge and conversation of the A∴A∴!

Witness my hand [old motto] _____

New Motto _____

The Task of a Zelator

0. Let any Neophyte who has accomplished his task to the satisfaction of the A∴A∴ be instructed in the proper course of procedure: which is:—Let him read through this note of his office, and sign it, paying the sum of Three Guineas for the volume containing Liber CCXX, Liber XXVII and Liber DCCCXIII, which will be given him on his initiation. Let him cause the necessary addition to be made to his Neophyte's robe, and entrust the same to the care of his Zelator. Let him make an appointment with his Zelator at the pleasure of the latter for the ceremony of initiation.

1. The Zelator shall proceed to the grade of Practicus at any time that authority confers it.

2. He shall pass Examinations in Liber E, Posture and Breathing. He shall have attained complete success in the former, i.e., the chosen posture shall be perfectly steady and easy; and attained the second stage in the latter, i.e., automatic rigidity.

3. He shall further show some acquaintance with and experience of the meditations given in Liber HHH. And in this his Record shall be his witness.

4. He shall commit to memory a chapter of Liber CCXX; he shall pass examinations in Liber HHH.

5. Beside all this, he shall apply himself to work for the A∴A∴ upon his own responsibility. Let him be mindful that the word Zelator is no idle term; but that a certain Zeal will be inflamed within him, why he knoweth not.

6. When authority confers the grade, he shall rejoice therein; but beware, for that is his first departure from the middle pillar of the Tree of Life.

7. He may at any moment withdraw from his association with the A∴A∴, simply notifying the Practicus who introduced him. Yet let him remember that being entered thus far upon the Path, he cannot escape it, and return to the world, but must ultimate either in the City of the Pyramids or the lonely towers of the Abyss.

8. He shall everywhere proclaim openly his connection with the A∴A∴ and speak of It and Its principles (even so little as he understandeth) for that mystery is the enemy of truth. Furthermore, he shall construct the magic Dagger, according to the instruction in Liber A. One month after his admission to the Grade he shall go to his Practicus, pass the necessary tests, and repeat to him his chosen chapter of Liber CCXX.

9. He shall in every way establish perfect control of his Automatic Consciousness according to the advice of his Practicus, for that the ordeal of advancement is no light one.

10. Thus and not otherwise may he attain the great reward, YEA, MAY HE ATTAIN THE GREAT REWARD!

The Oath of a Zelator

I, _____ (motto), being of sound mind and body, and prepared, on this ____ day of _____ [An ____ ☉ in _____ ° of _____] do hereby resolve: in the Presence of _____, a Practicus of the A∴A∴:

To prosecute the Great Work: which is, to obtain control of the foundations of my own being.

Further, I promise to observe zeal in service to the Neophytes under me, and to deny myself utterly on their behalf.

May the A∴A∴ crown the work, lend me of Its wisdom in the work, enable me to understand the work!

Reverence, duty, sympathy, devotion, assiduity do I bring to the A∴A∴ and right soon may I be admitted to the knowledge and conversation of the A∴A∴!

Witness my hand [motto] _____

The Task of a Practicus

0. Let any Zelator be appointed by authority to proceed to the grade of Practicus. Let him then read through this note of his office, and sign it. Let him cause the necessary addition to be made to his Zelator's robe. Let him make an appointment with his Practicus at the pleasure of the latter for the conferring of advancement.

1. The Practicus shall proceed to the grade of Philosophus at any time that authority confers it.

2. He shall pass examinations in Liber DCCLXXVII, the Qabalah, and the Sepher Sephiroth. He shall attain complete success in Liber III, Cap I.

3. He shall further show some acquaintance with and experience of his chosen method of divination. Yet he shall be his own judge in this matter.

4. He shall commit to memory Liber XXVII and pass examinations in the Ritual and meditation practice given in Liber XVI. Further, he shall pass the meditation practice S.S.S., in Liber HHH.

5. Besides all this, he shall apply himself to a way of life wholly suited to the Path. Let him remember that the word Practicus is no idle term, but that Action is the equilibrium of him that is in the House of Mercury, who is the Lord of Intelligence.

6. When authority confers the grade, he shall rejoice therein; but beware, for that that is his second departure from the middle pillar of the Tree of Life.

7. Let him not venture while a member of the grade of Practicus to attempt to withdraw from his association with the A∴A∴

8. He shall everywhere proclaim openly his connection with the A∴A∴ and speak of It and Its principles (even so little as he understandeth)

for that mystery is the enemy of truth. Furthermore, he shall construct the magic Cup, according to the instruction in Liber A. One month after his admission to the Grade, he shall go to his Philosophus, pass the necessary tests, and repeat to him Liber XXVII.

9. He shall in every way establish perfect control of his wit according to the advice of his Philosophus, for that the ordeal of advancement is no light one.

10. Thus and not otherwise may he attain the great reward, YEA, MAY HE ATTAIN THE GREAT REWARD!

The Oath of a Practicus

I, _____ (motto), being of sound mind and body, and prepared, on this _____ day of _____ [An _____ ☉ in _____ ° of _____] do hereby resolve: in the Presence of _____, a Philosophus of the A∴A∴:

To prosecute the Great Work: which is, to obtain control of the vacillations of my own being.

Further, I promise to observe zeal in service to the Zelatores under me, and to deny myself utterly on their behalf.

May the A∴A∴ crown the work, lend me of Its wisdom in the work, enable me to understand the work!

Reverence, duty, sympathy, devotion do I bring to the A∴A∴ and right soon may I be admitted to the knowledge and conversation of the A∴A∴!

Witness my hand [motto] _____

The Task of a Philosophus

0. Let any Practicus be appointed by authority to proceed to the grade of Philosophus. Let him then read through this note of his office, and sign it. Let him cause the necessary addition to be made to his Practicus' robe. Let him make an appointment with his Philosophus at the pleasure of the latter for the conferring of advancement.

1. The Philosophus shall proceed to the grade of Dominus Liminis at any time that authority confers it.

2. He shall pass examinations in Liber CLXXV and in Construction and Consecration of Talismans and in Evocation. Yet in this matter he shall be his own judge. He shall moreover attain complete success in Liber III, Cap. II. Further, he shall apply himself to study and practice the meditations given in Liber V.

3. He shall further show some acquaintance with and experience of Liber O, Caps. V, VI. Whereof his Record shall be his witness.

4. He shall commit to memory a chapter of Liber DCCCXIII.

5. Besides all this, he shall make constant and profound reflections upon the Path. Let him remember that the word Philosophus is no idle term, but that Philosophy is the Equilibrium of him that is in the house of Venus that is the Lady of Love.

6. When the title of Dominus Liminis is conferred upon him, let him rejoice exceedingly therein; but beware, for that it is but the false veil of the moon that hangs beneath the Sun.

7. Let him not venture while a member of the grade of Philosophus to attempt to withdraw from his association with the A∴A∴

8. He shall everywhere proclaim openly his connection with the A∴A∴ and speak of It and Its principles (even so little as he understandeth) for that mystery is the enemy of truth. Furthermore, he shall construct

the magic Wand, according to the instruction in Liber A. One month after his admission to the Grade, he shall go to his Dominus Liminis, pass the necessary tests, and repeat to him his chosen chapter of Liber DCCCXIII.

9. He shall in every way establish perfect control of his devotion according to the advice of his Dominus Liminis, for that the ordeal of advancement is no light one.

10. Thus and not otherwise may he attain the great reward, YEA, MAY HE ATTAIN THE GREAT REWARD!

The Oath of a Philosophus

I, _____ (motto), being of sound mind and body, and prepared, on this _____ day of _____ [An _____ ☉ in _____ ° of _____] do hereby resolve: in the Presence of _____, a Dominus Liminis of the A∴A∴:

To prosecute the Great Work: which is, to obtain control of the attractions and repulsions of my own being.

Further, I promise to observe zeal in service to the Practici under me, and to deny myself utterly on their behalf.

May the A∴A∴ crown the work, lend me of Its wisdom in the work, enable me to understand the work!

Reverence, duty, sympathy do I bring to the A∴A∴ and right soon may I be admitted to the knowledge and conversation of the A∴A∴!

Witness my hand [motto] _____

The Task of a Dominus Liminis

0. Let any Philosophus be appointed by authority a Dominus Liminis. Let him read through this note of his office and sign it. Let him cause the necessary addition to be made to his Philosophus' robe. Let him receive Liber Mysteriorum. Let him make an appointment with his Dominus Liminis at the pleasure of the latter for the conferring of advancement.

1. The Dominus Liminis shall proceed to the Grade of Adeptus Minor at any time that authority confers it.

2. He shall pass examination in Liber III, Cap. III.

3. He shall meditate on the diverse knowledge and Power that he has acquired, and harmonize it perfectly. And in this matter he shall be judged by the Præmonstrator of the A∴A∴

4. He shall accept an office in a Temple of Initiation, and commit to memory a part appointed by the Imperator of the A∴A∴

5. Besides all this, he shall abide on the Threshold. Let him remember that the word Dominus Liminis is no idle term, but that his mastery will often be disputed, when he knoweth it not.

6. When at last he hath attained to the grade of Adeptus Minor, let him humble himself exceedingly.

7. He may at any moment withdraw from his association with the A∴A∴ simply notifying the Adept who introduced him.

8. He shall everywhere proclaim openly his connection with the A∴A∴ and speak of It and Its principles (even so little as he understandeth) for that mystery is the enemy of truth. Furthermore, he shall construct the magic Lamp, according to the instruction in Liber A. Six months after his admission to the Grade, he shall go to his Adeptus Minor,

pass the necessary tests, and repeat to him his appointed part in the Temple of Initiation.

9. He shall in every way establish perfect control of his intuition, according to the advice of his Adeptus Minor, for that the ordeal of advancement is no light one.

10. Thus and not otherwise may he attain the great reward, YEA, MAY HE ATTAIN THE GREAT REWARD!

The Oath of a Dominus Liminis

I, _____ (motto), being of sound mind and body, and prepared, on this _____ day of _____ [An _____ ☉ in _____ ° of _____] do hereby resolve: in the Presence of _____, an Adeptus Minor of the A∴A∴:

To prosecute the Great Work: which is, to obtain control of the aspirations of my own being.

Further, I promise to observe zeal in service to the Philosophi under me, and to deny myself utterly on their behalf.

May the A∴A∴ crown the work, lend me of Its wisdom in the work, enable me to understand the work!

Reverence, duty, sympathy do I bring to the A∴A∴ and right soon may I be admitted to the knowledge and conversation of the A∴A∴!

Witness my hand [motto] _____

The Task of an Adeptus Minor

Let the Adeptus Minor attain to the Knowledge

and Conversation of his Holy Guardian Angel.

The Oath of an Adeptus Minor

I, _____ (motto), being of sound mind and body, and
prepared, on this ____ day of _____ [An ____ ☉ in _____
° of _____] do hereby resolve: in the Presence of
_____, an Adeptus of the A∴A∴:

To prosecute the Great Work: which is, to attain to the knowledge and
conversation of the Holy Guardian Angel.

May the A∴A∴ crown the work, lend me of Its wisdom in the work,
enable me to understand the work!

Reverence, duty, sympathy do I bring to the A∴A∴ and here and now
may I be admitted to the knowledge and conversation of the A∴A∴!

Witness my hand _____

II.

LIBER CAUSÆ

LIBER LXI

The Preliminary Lection
Including the History Lection

V

A∴A∴

Publication in Class D

THE PRELIMINARY
LECTION

In the name of the Initiator, Amen.

1. In the beginning was Initiation. The flesh profiteth nothing; the mind profiteth nothing; that which is unknown to you and above these, while firmly based upon their equilibrium, giveth life.

2. In all systems of religion is to be found a system of Initiation, which may be defined as the process whereby a man comes to learn that unknown Crown.

3. Though none can communicate either the knowledge or the power to achieve this, which we may call the Great Work, it is yet possible for initiates to guide others.

4. Every man must overcome his own obstacles, expose his own illusions. Yet others may assist him to do both, and they may enable him altogether to avoid many of the false paths, leading no whither, which tempt the weary feet of the uninitiated pilgrim. They can further insure that he is duly tried and tested, for there are many who think themselves to be Master who have not even begun to tread the Way of Service that leads thereto.

5. Now the Great Work is one, and the Initiation is one, and the Reward is one, however diverse are the symbols wherein the Unutterable is clothed.

6. Hear then the history of the system which this lection gives you the opportunity of investigating.

Listen, we pray you, with attention: for once only does the Great Order knock at any one door.

Whosoever knows any member of that Order as such, can never know another, until he too has attained to mastery.

Here, therefore, we pause, that you may thoroughly search yourself, and consider if you are yet fitted to take an irrevocable step.

For the reading of that which follows is Recorded.

THE HISTORY LECTION

7. Some years ago a number of cipher MSS. were discovered and deciphered by certain students. They attracted much attention, as they purported to derive from the Rosicrucians. You will readily understand that the genuineness of the claim matters no whit, such literature being judged by itself, not by its reputed sources.

8. Among the MSS. was one which gave the address of a certain person in Germany, who is known to us as S.D.A. Those who discovered the ciphers wrote to S.D.A., and in accordance with instructions received, an Order was founded which worked in a semi-secret manner.

9. After some time S.D.A. died: further requests for help were met with a prompt refusal from the colleagues of S.D.A. It was written by one of them that S.D.A.'s scheme had always been regarded with disapproval. But since the absolute rule of the adepts is never to interfere with the judgements of any other person whomsoever—how much more, then, one of themselves, and that one most highly revered!—they had refrained from active opposition. The adept who wrote this added that the Order had already quite enough knowledge to enable it or its members to formulate a magical link with the adepts.

10. Shortly after this, one called S.R.M.D. announced that he had formulated such a link, and that himself and two others were to govern the Order. New and revised rituals were issued, and fresh knowledge poured out in streams.

11. We must pass over the unhappy juggleries which characterised the next period. It has throughout proved impossible to elucidate the complex facts. We content ourselves, then, with observing that the death of one of his two colleagues, and the weakness of the other, secured to S.R.M.D. the sole authority. The rituals were elaborated, though scholarly enough, into verbose and pretentious nonsense: the knowledge proved worthless even where it was correct: for it is in vain that pearls, be they never so clear and precious, are given to the swine.

The ordeals were turned into contempt, it being impossible for anyone to fail therein. Unsuitable candidates were admitted for no better reason than that of their worldly prosperity. In short, the Order failed to initiate.

12. Scandal arose, and with it schism.

13. In 1900, one P., a brother, instituted a rigorous test of S.R.M.D. on the one side and the Order on the other.

14. He discovered that S.R.M.D., though a scholar of some ability and a magician of remarkable powers, had never attained complete initiation: and further had fallen from his original place, he having imprudently attracted to himself forces of evil too great and terrible for him to withstand. The claim of the Order that the true adepts were in charge of it was definitely disproved.

15. In the Order, with two certain exceptions and two doubtful ones, he found no persons prepared for initiation of any sort.

16. He thereupon by his subtle wisdom destroyed both the Order and its chief.

17. Being himself no perfect adept, he was driven of the Spirit into the Wilderness, where he abode for six years, studying by the light of reason the sacred books and secret systems of all countries and ages.

18. Finally, there was given unto him a certain exalted grade whereby a man becomes master of knowledge and intelligence, and no more their slave. He perceived the inadequacy of science, philosophy, and religion; and exposed the self-contradictory nature of the thinking faculty.

19. Returning to England, he laid his achievements humbly at the feet of a certain adept D.D.S., who welcomed him brotherly and admitted his title to the grade which he had so hardly won.

20. Thereupon these two adepts conferred together, saying: May it not be written that the tribulations shall be shortened? Wherefore they

resolved to establish a new Order which should be free from the errors and deceits of the former one.

21. Without Authority they could not do this, exalted as their rank was among adepts. They resolved to prepare all things, great and small, against that day when such Authority should be received by them, since they knew not where to seek for higher adepts than themselves, but knew that the true way to attract the notice of such was to equilibrate the symbols. The temple must be builded before the God can indwell it.

22. Therefore by the order of D.D.S. did P. prepare all things by his arcane science and wisdom, choosing only those symbols which were common to all systems, and rigorously rejecting all names and words which might be supposed to imply any religious or metaphysical theory. To do this utterly was found impossible, since all language has a history, and the use (for example) of the word "spirit" implies the Scholastic Philosophy and the Hindu and Taoist theories concerning the breath of man. So was it difficult to avoid implication of some undesirable bias by using the words "order," "circle," "chapter," "society," "brotherhood," or any other to designate the body of initiates.

23. Deliberately, therefore, did he take refuge in vagueness. Not to veil the truth to the Neophyte, but to warn him against valuing non-essentials. Should therefore the candidate hear the name of any God, let him not rashly assume that it refers to any known God, save only the God known to himself. Or should the ritual speak in terms (however vague) which seem to imply Egyptian, Taoist, Buddhist, Indian, Persian, Greek, Judaic, Christian or Moslem philosophy, let him reflect that this is a defect of language, the literary limitation and not the spiritual prejudice of the man P.

24. Especially let him guard against the finding of definite sectarian symbols in the teaching of his master, and the reasoning from the known to the unknown which assuredly will tempt him. We labour earnestly, dear brother, that you may never be led away to perish upon

this point; for thereon have many holy and just men been wrecked. By this have all the visible systems lost the essence of wisdom. We have sought to reveal the Arcanum; we have only profaned it.

25. Now when P. had thus with bitter toil prepared all things under the guidance of D.D.S. (even as the hand writes, while the conscious brain, though ignorant of the detailed movements, applauds or disapproves the finished work) there was a certain period of repose, as the earth lieth fallow.

26. Meanwhile these adepts busied themselves intently with the Great Work.

27. In the fullness of time, even as a blossoming tree that beareth fruit in its season, all these pains were ended, and these adepts and their companions obtained the reward which they had sought—they were to be admitted to the Eternal and Invisible Order that hath no name among men.

28. They therefore who had with smiling faces abandoned their homes, their possessions, their wives, their children, in order to perform the Great Work, could with steady calm and firm correctness abandon the Great Work itself; for this is the last and greatest projection of the alchemist.

29. Also one V.V.V.V.V. arose, an exalted adept of the rank of Master of the Temple (or this much He disclosed to the Exempt Adepts) and His utterance is enshrined in the Sacred Writings.

30. Such are Liber Legis, Liber Cordis Cincti Serpente, Liber Liberi vel Lapidis Lazuli and such others whose existence may one day be divulged to you. Beware lest you interpret them either in the Light or the darkness, for only in L.V.X. may they be understood.

31. Also He conferred upon D.D.S., O.M., and another, the Authority of the Triad, who in turn have delegated it unto others, and they yet again, so that the Body of Initiates may be perfect, even from the Crown unto the Kingdom and beyond.

32. For Perfection abideth not in the Pinnacles, or in the Foundations, but in the ordered Harmony of one with all.

III.

AN ACCOUNT OF A∴A∴

LIBER XXXIII

First written in the Language of his Period

by the Councillor Von Eckartshausen

and now revised and rewritten in the

Universal Cipher

V

A∴A∴

[The Revisers wish to acknowledge gratefully the translation of Madame de Steiger, which they have freely quoted.]
IT is necessary, my dear brothers, to give you a clear idea of the interior Order; of that illuminated community which is scattered throughout the world, but which is governed by one truth and united in one spirit.

This community possesses a School, in which all who thirst for knowledge are instructed by the Spirit of Wisdom itself; and all the mysteries of nature are preserved in this school for the children of light. Perfect knowledge of nature and of humanity is taught in this school. It is from her that all truths penetrate into the world; she is the school of all who search for wisdom, and it is in this community alone that truth and the explanation of all mystery are to be found. It is the most hidden of communities, yet it contains members from many circles; nor is there any Centre of Thought whose activity is not due to the presence of one of ourselves. From all time there has been an exterior school based on the interior one, of which it is but the outer expression. From all time, therefore, there has been a hidden assembly, a society of the Elect, of those who sought for and had capacity for light, and this interior society was the Axle of the R.O.T.A. All that any external order possesses in symbol, ceremony, or rite is the letter expressive outwardly of that spirit of truth which dwelleth in the interior Sanctuary. Nor is the contradiction of the exterior any bar to the harmony of the interior.

Hence this Sanctuary, composed of members widely scattered indeed but united by the bonds of perfect love, has been occupied from the earliest ages in building the grand Temple (through the evolution of humanity) by which the reign of L.V.X. will be manifest. This society is in the communion of those who have most capacity for light; they are united in truth, and their Chief is the Light of the World himself, V.V.V.V.V., the One Anointed in Light, the single teacher for the human race, the Way, the Truth, and the Life.

The interior Order was formed immediately after the first perception of man's wider heritage had dawned upon the first of the adepts; it received from the Masters at first-hand the revelation of the means by which humanity could be raised to its rights and delivered from its misery. It received the primitive charge of all revelation and mystery; it received the key of true science, both divine and natural.
But as men multiplied, the frailty of man necessitated an exterior society which veiled the interior one, and concealed the spirit and the truth in the letter, because many people were not capable of comprehending great interior truth. Therefore, interior truths were wrapped in external and perceptible ceremonies, so that men, by the perception of the outer which is the symbol of the interior, might by degrees be enabled safely to approach the interior spiritual truths.

But the inner truth has always been confided to him who in his day had the most capacity for illumination, and he became the sole guardian of the original Trust, as High Priest of the Sanctuary.

When it became necessary that interior truths should be enfolded in exterior ceremony and symbol, on account of the real weakness of men who were not capable of hearing the Light of Light, then exterior worship began. It was, however, always the type or symbol of the interior, that is to say, the symbol of the true and Secret Sacrament. The external worship would never have been separated from interior revel but for the weakness of man, which tends too easily to forget the spirit in the letter; but the Masters are vigilant to note in every nation those who are able to receive light, and such persons are employed as agents to spread the light according to man's capacity and to revivify the dead letter.

Through these instruments the interior truths of the Sanctuary were taken into every nation, and modified symbolically according to their customs, capacity for instruction, climate, and receptiveness. So that the external types of every religion, worship, ceremonies and Sacred Books in general have more or less clearly, as their object of instruction, the interior truths of the Sanctuary, by which man will be conducted to the universal knowledge of the one Absolute Truth. The more the external worship of a people has remained united with the spirit of esoteric truth, the purer its religion; but the wider the difference between the symbolic letter and the invisible truth, the more imperfect has become the religion. Finally, it may be, the external form has entirely parted from its inner truth, so that ceremonial observances without soul or life have remained alone.

In the midst of all this, truth reposes inviolable in the inner Sanctuary. Faithful to the spirit of truth, the members of the interior Order live in silence, but in real activity. Yet, besides their secret holy work, they have from time to time decided upon political strategic action. Thus, when the earth was nigh utterly corrupt by reason of the Great Sorcery, the Brethren sent Mohammed to bring freedom to mankind by the sword. This being but partially a success, they raised up one Luther to teach freedom of thought. Yet this freedom soon turned into a heavier bondage than before.

Then the Brethren delivered unto man the knowledge of nature, and the keys thereof; yet this also was prevented by the Great Sorcery. Now then finally in nameless ways, as one of our Brethren hath it now in mind to declare, have they raised up One to deliver unto men the keys of Spiritual Knowledge, and by His work shall He be judged. This interior community of light is the reunion of all those capable of receiving light, and it is known as the Communion of Saints, the primitive receptacle for all strength and truth, confided to it from all time.

By it the agents of L.V.X. were formed in every age, passing from the interior to the exterior, and communicating spirit and life to the dead letter, as already said. This illuminated community is the true school of L.V.X.; it has its Chair, its Doctors; it possesses a rule for students; it has forms and objects for study. It has also its degrees for successive development to greater altitudes. This school of wisdom has been for ever most secretly hidden from the world, because it is invisible and submissive solely to illuminated government.

It has never been exposed to the accidents of time and to the weakness of man, because only the most capable were chosen for it, and those who selected made no error. Through this school were developed the germs of all the sublime sciences, which were first received by external schools, then clothed in other forms, and hence degenerated.

According to time and circumstances, the society of sages communicated unto the exterior societies their symbolic hieroglyphs, in order to attract man to the great truths of their Sanctuary.
But all exterior societies subsist only by virtue of this interior one. As soon as external societies wish to transform a temple of wisdom into a political edifice, the interior society retires and leaves only the letter without the spirit. It is thus that secret external societies of wisdom

were nothing but hieroglyphic screens, the truth remaining inviolable in the Sanctuary so that she might never be profaned.

In this interior society man finds wisdom and with her All—not the wisdom of this world, which is but scientific knowledge, which revolves round the outside but never touches the centre (in which is contained all strength), but true wisdom, understanding and knowledge, reflections of the supreme illumination.
All disputes, all controversies, all the things belonging to the false cares of this world, fruitless discussions, useless germs of opinions which spread the seeds of disunion, all error, schisms, and systems are banished. Neither calumny nor scandal is known. Every man is honoured. Love alone reigns.

We must not, however, imagine that this society resembles any secret society, meeting at certain times, choosing leaders and members, united by special objects. All societies, be what they may, can but come after this interior illuminated circle. This society knows none of the formalities which belong to the outer rings, the work of man. In this kingdom of power all outward forms cease.
L.V.X. is the Power always present. The greatest man of his times, the chief himself, does not always know all the members, but the moment when it is necessary that he should accomplish any object he finds them in the world with certainty ready to his hand.

This community has no outside barriers. He who may be chosen is as the first; he presents himself among the others without presumption, and he is received by the others without jealousy.
If it be necessary that real members should meet together, they find and recognize each other with perfect certainty.

No disguise can be used, neither hypocrisy nor dissimulation could hide the characteristic qualities which distinguish the members of this society. All illusion is gone, and things appear in their true form.

No one member can choose another; unanimous choice is required. Though not all men are called, many of the called are chosen, and that as soon as they become fit for entrance.

Any man can look for the entrance, and any man who is within can teach another to seek for it; but only he who is fit can arrive within. Unprepared men occasion disorder in a community, and disorder is not compatible with the Sanctuary. Thus it is impossible to profane the Sanctuary, since admission is not formal but real.
Worldly intelligence seeks this Sanctuary in vain; fruitless also will be the efforts of malice to penetrate these great mysteries; all is indecipherable to him who is not ripe; he can see nothing, read nothing in the interior.

He who is fit is joined to the chain, perhaps often where he thought least likely, and at a point of which he knew nothing himself.
To become fit should be the sole effort of him who seeks wisdom. But there are methods by which fitness is attained, for in this holy communion is the primitive storehouse of the most ancient and original science of the human race, with the primitive mysteries also of all science. It is the unique and really illuminated community which is absolutely in possession of the key to all mystery, which knows the centre and source of all nature. It is a society which unites superior strength to its own, and counts its members from more than one world. It is the society whose members form the republic of Genius, the Regent Mother of the whole World.

IV.

LIBER E

VEL
EXERCITIORVM
SVB FIGVRÂ IX

V

A∴A∴

Publication in Class B

Issued by Order:
D.D.S. 7°=4° Præmonstrator
O.S.V. 6°=5° Imperator
N.S.F. 5°=6° Cancellarius

I

1. It is absolutely necessary that all experiments should be recorded in detail during, or immediately after, their performance.

2. It is highly important to note the physical and mental condition of the experimenter or experimenters.

3. The time and place of all experiments must be noted; also the state of the weather, and generally all conditions which might conceivably have any result upon the experiment either as adjuvants to or causes of the result, or as inhibiting it, or as sources of error.

4. The A∴A∴ will not take official notice of any experiments which are not thus properly recorded.

5. It is not necessary at this stage for us to declare fully the ultimate end of our researches; nor indeed would it be understood by those who have not become proficient in these elementary courses.

6. The experimenter is encouraged to use his own intelligence, and not to rely upon any other person or persons, however distinguished, even among ourselves.

7. The written record should be intelligibly prepared so that others may benefit from its study.

8. The book John St. John published in the first number of the "Equinox" is an example of this kind of record by a very advanced student. It is not as simply written as we could wish, but will shew the method.

9. The more scientific the record is, the better. Yet the emotions should be noted, as being some of the conditions. Let then the record be written with sincerity and care, and with practice it will be found more and more to approximate to the ideal.

II

Physical Clairvoyance

1. Take a pack of (78) Tarot playing cards. Shuffle; cut. Draw one card. Without looking at it, try and name it. Write down the card you name, and the actual card. Repeat, and tabulate results.

2. This experiment is probably easier with an old genuine pack of Tarot cards, preferably a pack used for divination by some one who really understood the matter.

3. Remember that one should expect to name the right card once in 78 times. Also be careful to exclude all possibilities of obtaining the knowledge through the ordinary senses of sight and touch, or even smell. There was once a man whose finger-tips were so sensitive that he could feel the shape and position of the pips, and so judge the card correctly.

4. It is better to try first, the easier form of the experiment, by guessing only the suit.

5. Remember that in 78 experiments you should obtain 22 trumps and 14 of each other suit; so that, without any clairvoyance at all, you can guess right twice in 7 times (roughly) by calling trumps each time.

6. Note that some cards are harmonious. Thus it would not be a bad error to call the five of Swords ("The Lord of Defeat") instead of the ten of Swords ("The Lord of Ruin"). But to call the Lord of Love (2 Cups) for the Lord of Strife (5 Wands) would show that you were getting nothing right. Similarly, a card ruled by Mars would be harmonious with a 5, a card of Gemini with "The Lovers."

7. These harmonies must be thoroughly learnt, according to the numerous tables given in 777.

8. As you progress, you will find that you are able to distinguish the suit correctly three times in four, and that very few indeed inharmonious errors occur, while in 78 experiments you are able to name the card aright as many as 15 or 20 times.

9. When you have reached this stage, you may be admitted for examination; and in the event of your passing, you will be given more complex and difficult exercises.

III

Asana — Posture

1. You must learn to sit perfectly still with every muscle tense for long periods.

2. You must wear no garment that interferes with the posture in any of these experiments.

3. The first position: (The God). Sit in a chair; head up, back straight, knees together, hands on knees, eyes closed.

4. The second position: (The Dragon). Kneel; buttocks resting on the heels, toes turned back, back and head straight, hands on thighs.

5. The third position: (The Ibis). Stand; hold left ankle with right hand (and alternately practise right ankle in left hand, &c.) free forefinger on lips.

6. The fourth position: (The Thunderbolt). Sit: left heel pressing up anus, right foot poised on its toes, the heel covering the phallus; arms stretched out over the knees: head and back straight.

THE FOUR POSITIONS

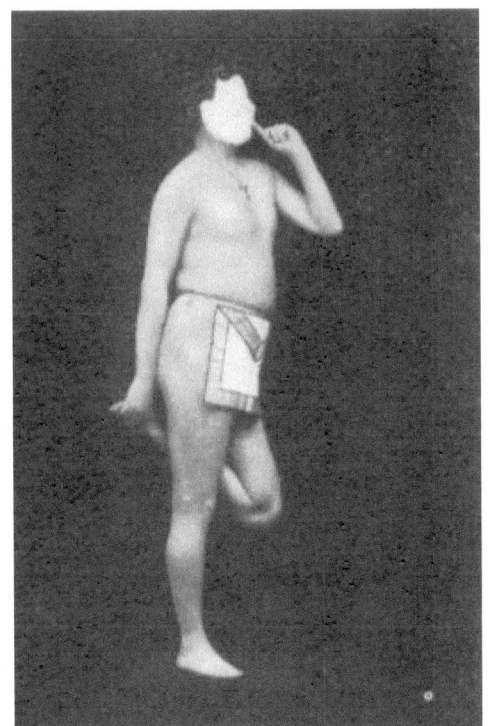

The Ibis

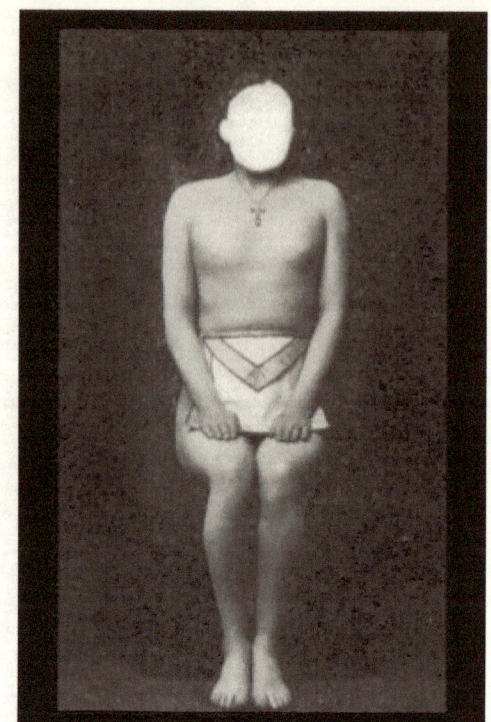

The God

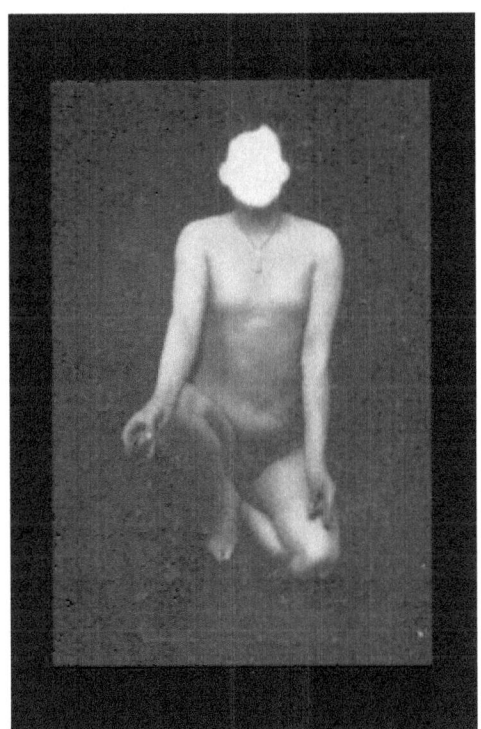

The Thunderbolt

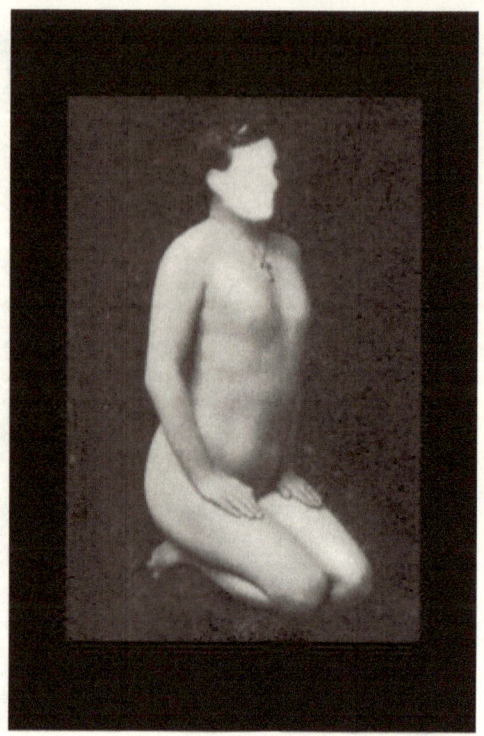

The Dragon

In the Ibis the head is tilted very slightly too far back; in the Thunderbolt the right foot might be a little higher and the right knee lower with advantage.

7. Various things will happen to you while you are practising these positions; they must be carefully analysed and described.

8. Note down the duration of the practice, the severity of the pain (if any) which accompanies it, the degree of rigidity attained, and any other pertinent matters.

9. When you have progressed up to the point that a saucer filled to the brim with water and poised upon the head does not spill one drop during a whole hour, and when you can no longer perceive the slightest tremor in any muscle; when, in short, you are perfectly steady and easy, you will be admitted for examination; and, should you pass, you will be instructed in more complex and difficult practices.

IV

Pranayama — Regularisation of the Breathing

1. At rest in one of your positions, close the right nostril with the thumb of the right hand and breathe out slowly and completely through the left nostril, while your watch marks 20 seconds. Breathe in through the same nostril for 10 seconds. Changing hands, repeat with the other nostril. Let this be continuous for one hour.

2. When this is quite easy to you, increase the periods to 30 and 15 seconds.

3. When this is quite easy to you, but not before, breathe out for 15 seconds, in for 15 seconds, and hold the breath for 15 seconds.

4. When you can do this with perfect ease and comfort for a whole hour, practise breathing out for 40, in for 20 seconds.

5. This being attained, practise breathing out for 20, in for 10, holding the breath for 30 seconds. When this has become perfectly easy to you, you may be admitted for examination, and should you pass, you will be instructed in more complex and difficult practices.

6. You will find that the presence of food in the stomach, even in small quantities, makes the practices very difficult.

7. Be very careful never to overstrain your powers; especially never get so short of breath that you are compelled to breathe out jerkily or rapidly.

8. Strive after depth, fulness, and regularity of breathing.

9. Various remarkable phenomena will very probably occur during these practices. They must be carefully analysed and recorded.

V

Dharana — Control of Thought

1. Constrain the mind to concentrate itself upon a single simple object imagined. The five tatwas are useful for this purpose; they are: a black oval; a blue disk; a silver crescent; a yellow square; a red triangle.

2. Proceed to combinations of simple objects; e.g., a black oval within a yellow square, and so on.

3. Proceed to simple moving objects, such as a pendulum swinging, a wheel revolving, &c. Avoid living objects.

4. Proceed to combinations of moving objects, e.g., a piston rising and falling while a pendulum is swinging. The relation between the two movements should be varied in different experiments. Or even a system of fly-wheels, eccentrics, and governor.

5. During these practices the mind must be absolutely confined to the object determined upon; no other thought must be allowed to intrude upon the consciousness. The moving systems must be regular and harmonious.

6. Note carefully the duration of the experiments, the number and nature of the intruding thoughts, the tendency of the object itself to depart from the course laid out for it, and any other phenomena which may present themselves. Avoid overstrain. This is very important.

7. Proceed to imagine living objects; as a man, preferably some man known to, and respected by, yourself.

8. In the intervals of these experiments you may try to imagine the objects of the other senses, and to concentrate upon them. For example, try to imagine the taste of chocolate, the smell of roses, the feeling of velvet, the sound of a waterfall, or the ticking of a watch.

9. Endeavour finally to shut out all objects of any of the senses, and prevent all thoughts arising in your mind. When you feel that you have attained some success in these practices, apply for examination, and should you pass, more complex and difficult practices will be prescribed for you.

VI

Physical Limitations

1. It is desirable that you should discover for yourself your physical limitations.

2. To this end ascertain for how many hours you can subsist without food or drink before your working capacity is seriously interfered with.

3. Ascertain how much alcohol you can take, and what forms of drunkenness assail you.

4. Ascertain how far you can walk without once stopping; likewise with dancing, swimming, running, &c.

5. Ascertain for how many hours you can do without sleep.

6. Test your endurance with various gymnastic exercises, club-swinging and so on.

7. Ascertain for how long you can keep silence.

8. Investigate any other capacities and aptitudes which may occur to you.

9. Let all these things be carefully and conscientiously recorded; for according to your powers will it be demanded of you.

VII

A Course of Reading

1. The object of most of the foregoing practices will not at first be clear to you; but at least (who will deny it?) they will have trained you in determination, accuracy, introspection, and many other qualities which are valuable to all men in their ordinary avocations, so that in no case will your time have been wasted.

2. That you may gain some insight into the nature of the Great Work which lies beyond these elementary trifles, however, we should mention that an intelligent person may gather more than a hint of its nature from the following books, which are to be taken as serious and learned contributions to the study of nature, though not necessarily to be implicitly relied upon.

"The Yi King" [S.B.E. Series, Oxford University Press].

"The Tao Teh King" [S.B.E. Series].

"Tannhäuser" by A. Crowley.

"The Upanishads."

"The Bhagavad-Gita."

"The Voice of the Silence."

"Raja Yoga" by Swami Vivekananda.

"The Shiva Sanhita."

"The Aphorisms of Patanjali."

"The Sword of Song."

"The Book of the Dead."

"Rituel et Dogme de la Haute Magie."

"The Book of the Sacred Magic of Abramelin the Mage."

"The Goetia."

"The Hathayoga Pradipika."

Erdmann's "History of Philosophy."

"The Spiritual Guide of Molinos."

"The Star in the West" (Captain Fuller).

"The Dhammapada" [S.B.E. Series].

"The Questions of King Milinda" [S.B.E. Series].

"777. vel Prolegomena, &c."

"Varieties of Religious Experience" (James).

"Kabbala Denudata."

"Konx Om Pax."

3. Careful study of these books will enable the pupil to speak in the language of his master and facilitate communication with him.

4. The pupil should endeavour to discover the fundamental harmony of these very varied works; for this purpose he will find it best to study the most extreme divergences side by side.

5. He may at any time that he wishes apply for examination in this course of reading.

6. During the whole of this elementary study and practice, he will do wisely to seek out, and attach himself to, a master, one competent to correct him and advise him. Nor should he be discouraged by the difficulty of finding such a person.

7. Let him further remember that he must in no wise rely upon, or believe in, that master. He must rely entirely upon himself, and credit nothing whatever but that which lies within his own knowledge and experience.

8. As in the beginning, so at the end, we here insist upon the vital importance of the written record as the only possible check upon error derived from the various qualities of the experimenter.

9. Thus let the work be accomplished duly; yea, let it be accomplished duly.

SUPPLEMENTARY INSTRUCTION IN ASANA

Some of the weaker brethren having found the postures in Liber E too difficult, the pitiful heart of the Præmonstrator of A∴A∴ has been moved to authorise the publication of additional postures, which will be found below. An elderly, corpulent gentleman of sedentary habit has been good enough to pose, so that none need feel debarred from devoting himself to the Great Work on the ground of physical infirmity.

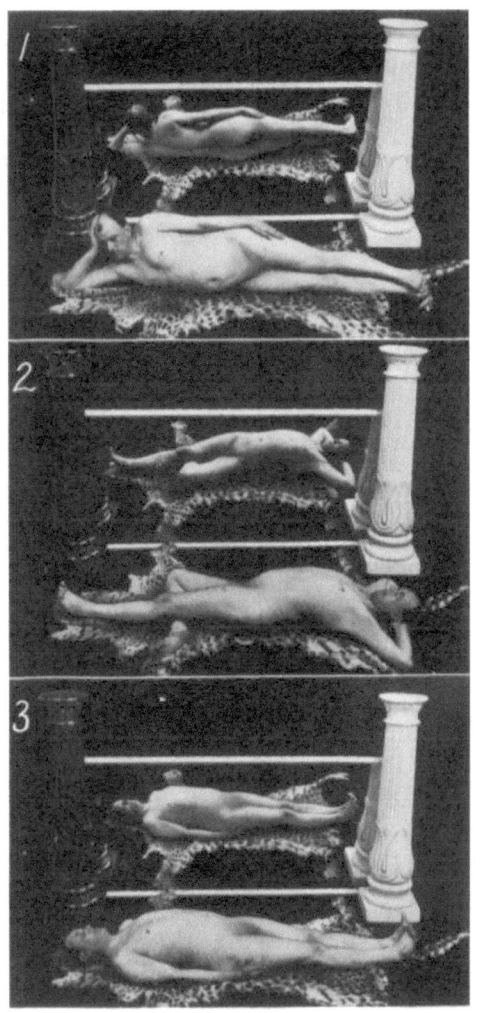

Recumbent Positions: 1. The Dying Buddha, 2. The Hanged Man, 3. The Corpse

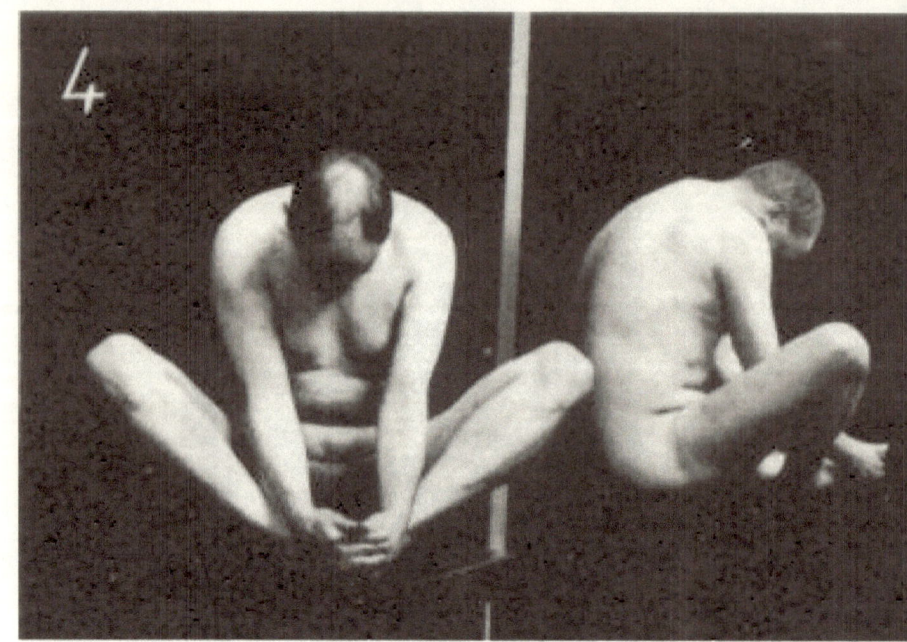

4. The Arrowhead

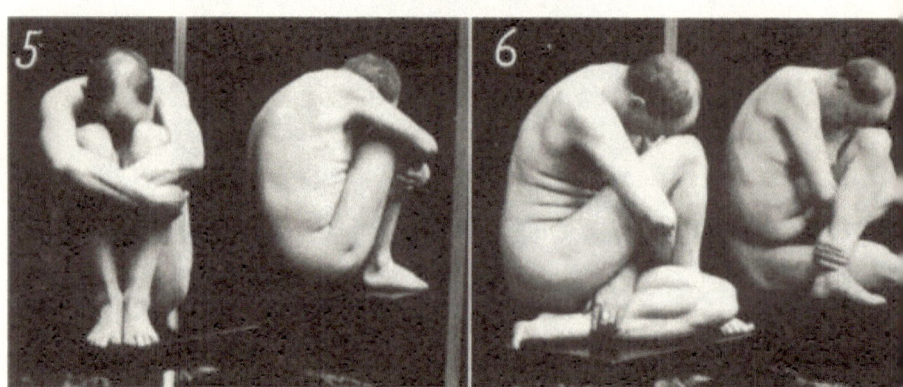

5. The Bear, 6. The Ivy

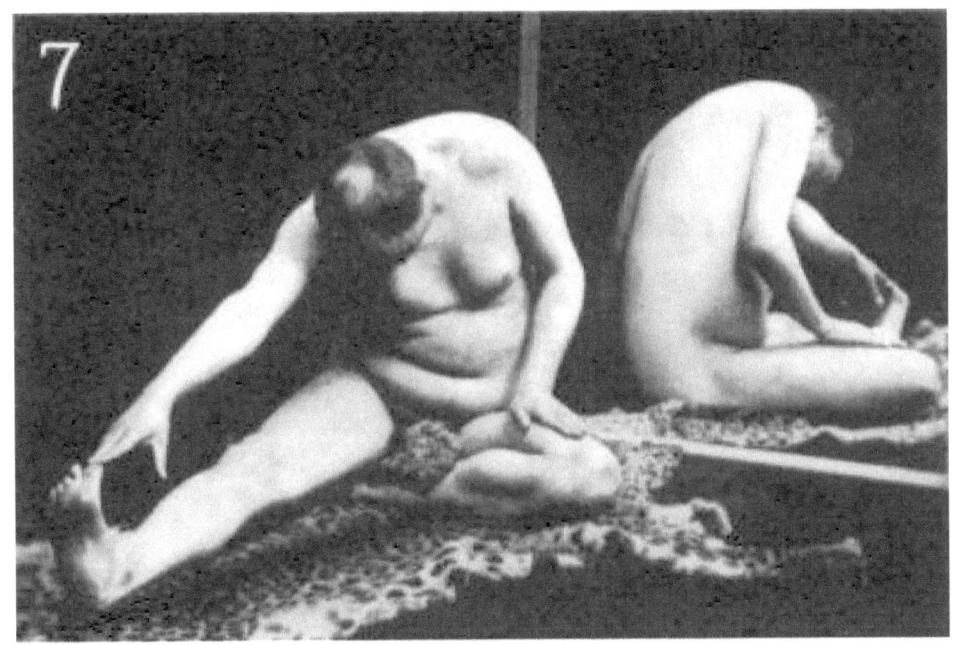

7. The Parallelogram

The recumbent positions (1-3) are more suitable for repose after meditations than for meditation itself. The positions with bowed head (4-7) are suitable for Asana and for meditation, but not for Pranayama.

[If any really important or remarkable results should occur, or if any great difficulty presents itself, the A∴A∴ should be at once informed of the circumstances.]

V.

LIBER O

VEL MANVS ET

SAGITTÆ SVB FIGVRÂ

VI

V

A∴A∴

Publication in Class B

Issued by Order:

D.D.S. 7°=4° Præmonstrator

O.S.V. 6°=5° Imperator

N.S.F. 5°=6° Cancellarius

I

1. This book is very easy to misunderstand; readers are asked to use the most minute critical care in the study of it, even as we have done in its preparation.

2. In this book it is spoken of the Sephiroth and the Paths; of Spirits and Conjurations; of Gods, Spheres, Planes, and many other things that may or may not exist. It is immaterial whether these exist or not. By doing certain things, certain results will follow; students are

earnestly warned against attributing objective reality or philosophical validity to any of them.

3. The advantages to be gained from them are chiefly these: (a) A widening of the horizon of the mind. (b) An improvement of the control of the mind.

4. The student, if he attain to success in the following practices, will find himself confronted by things (ideas or beings) too glorious or too dreadful to be described. It is essential that he remain the master of all that he beholds, hears or conceives; otherwise he will be the slave of illusion, and the prey of madness. Before entering upon any of these practices, the student should be in good health, and have attained a fair mastery of Asana, Pranayama, and Dharana.

5. There is little danger that any student, however idle or stupid, will fail to get some result; but there is great danger that he will be led astray, obsessed and overwhelmed by his results, even though it be by those which it is necessary that he should attain. Too often, moreover, he mistaketh the first resting-place for the goal, and taketh off his armour as if he were a victor ere the fight is well begun. It is desirable that the student should never attach to any result the importance which it at first seems to possess.

6. First, then, let us consider the Book 777 and its use; the preparation of the Place; the use of the Magic Ceremonies; and finally the methods which follow in Chapter V. "Viator in Regnis Arboris," and in Chapter VI. "Sagitta trans Lunam." (In another book will it be treated of the Expansion and Contraction of Consciousness; progress by slaying the Cakkrâms; progress by slaying the Pairs of Opposites; the methods of Sabhapaty Swami, &c. &c.)

II

1. The student must FIRST obtain a thorough knowledge of Book 777, especially of columns i., ii., iii., v., vi., vii., ix., xi., xii., xiv., xv., xvi., xvii., xviii., xix., xxxiv., xxxv., xxxviii., xxxix., xl., xli., xlii., xlv., liv., lv., lix., lx., lxi., lxiii., lxx., lxxv., lxxvii., lxxviii., lxxix., lxxx., lxxxi., lxxxiii., xcvii., xcviii., xcix., c., ci., cxvii., cxviii., cxxxvii., cxxxviii., cxxxix., clxxv., clxxvi., clxxvii., clxxxii. When these are committed to memory, he will begin to understand the nature of these correspondences.

2. If we take an example the use of the table will become clear. Let us suppose that you wish to obtain knowledge of some obscure science. In column xlv., line 12, you will find "Knowledge of Sciences." By now looking up line 12 in the other columns, you will find that the Planet corresponding is Mercury, its number eight, its lineal figures the octagon and octagram, the God who rules that planet Thoth, or in Hebrew symbolism Tetragrammaton Adonai and Elohim Tzabaoth, its Archangel Raphael, its Choir of Angels Beni Elohim, its Intelligence Tiriel, its Spirit Taphtatharath, its colours Orange (for Mercury is the sphere of the Sephira Hod, 8), Yellow, Purple, Grey, and Indigo rayed with Violet; its Magical Weapon the Wand or Caduceus, its Perfumes Mastic and others, its sacred plants Vervain and others, its jewel the Opal or Agate, its sacred animal the Snake, &c. &c.

3. You would then prepare your Place of Working accordingly. In an orange circle you would draw an eight-pointed star of yellow, at whose points you would place eight lamps. The Sigil of the Spirit (which is to be found in Cornelius Agrippa and other books) you would draw in the four colours with such other devices as your experiences may suggest.

4. And so on. We cannot here enter at length into all the necessary preparations; and the student will find them fully set forth in the proper books, of which the "Goetia" is perhaps the best example. These rituals need not be slavishly imitated; on the contrary the student should do nothing the object of which he does not understand; also, if he have any capacity whatever, he will find his own crude rituals more

effective than the highly polished ones of other people. The general purpose of all this preparation is as follows:

5. Since the student is a man surrounded by material objects, if it be his wish to master one particular idea, he must make every material object about him directly suggest that idea. Thus in the ritual quoted, if his glance fall upon the lights, their number suggests Mercury; he smells the perfumes, and again Mercury is brought to his mind. In other words, the whole magical apparatus and ritual is a complex system of mnemonics. [The importance of these lies principally in the fact that particular sets of images that the student may meet in his wanderings correspond to particular lineal figures, divine names, &c., and are controlled by them. As to possibility of producing results external to the mind of the seer (objective, in the ordinary common-sense acceptation of the term) we are here silent.]

6. There are three important practices connected with all forms of ceremonial (and the two Methods which later we shall describe). These are: (1) Assumption of God-forms. (2) Vibrations of Divine Names. (3) Rituals of "Banishing" and "Invoking." These, at least, should be completely mastered before the dangerous Methods of Chapters V. and VI. are attempted.

III

1. The Magical Images of the Gods of Egypt should be made thoroughly familiar. This can be done by studying them in any public museum, or in such books as may be accessible to the student. They should then be carefully painted by him, both from the model and from memory.

2. The student, seated in the "God" position, or in the characteristic attitude of the God desired, should then imagine His image as

coinciding with his own body, or as enveloping it. This must be practiced until mastery of the image is attained, and an identity with it and with the God experienced. It is a matter for very great regret that no simple and certain tests of success in this practice exist.

3. The vibration of God-names. As a further means of identifying the human consciousness with that pure portion of it which man calls by the name of some God, let him act thus:

4. (a) Stand with arms outstretched. (b) Breathe in deeply through the nostrils, imagining the name of the God desired entering with the breath. (c) Let that name descend slowly from the lungs to the heart, the solar plexus, the navel, the generative organs, and so to the feet. (d) The moment that it appears to touch the feet, quickly advance the left foot about twelve inches, throw forward the body, and let the hands (drawn back to the side of the eyes) shoot out, so that you are standing in the typical position of the God Horus, and at the same time imagine the Name as rushing up through the body, while you breathe it out through the nostrils with the air which has been till then retained in the lungs. All this must be done with all the force of which you are capable. (e) Then withdraw the left foot, and place the right forefinger upon the lips, so that you are in the characteristic position of the God Harpocrates.

5. It is a sign that the student is performing this correctly when a single "Vibration" entirely exhausts his physical strength. It should cause him to grow hot all over, or to perspire violently, and it should so weaken him that he will find it difficult to remain standing.

6. It is a sign of success, though only by the student himself is it perceived, when he hears the name of the God vehemently roared forth, as if by the concourse of ten thousand thunders; and it should appear to him as if that Great Voice proceeded from the Universe, and not from himself. In both the above practices all consciousness of anything but the God-form and name should be absolutely blotted out; and the longer it takes for normal perception to return, the better.

THE SIGNS OF THE GRADES

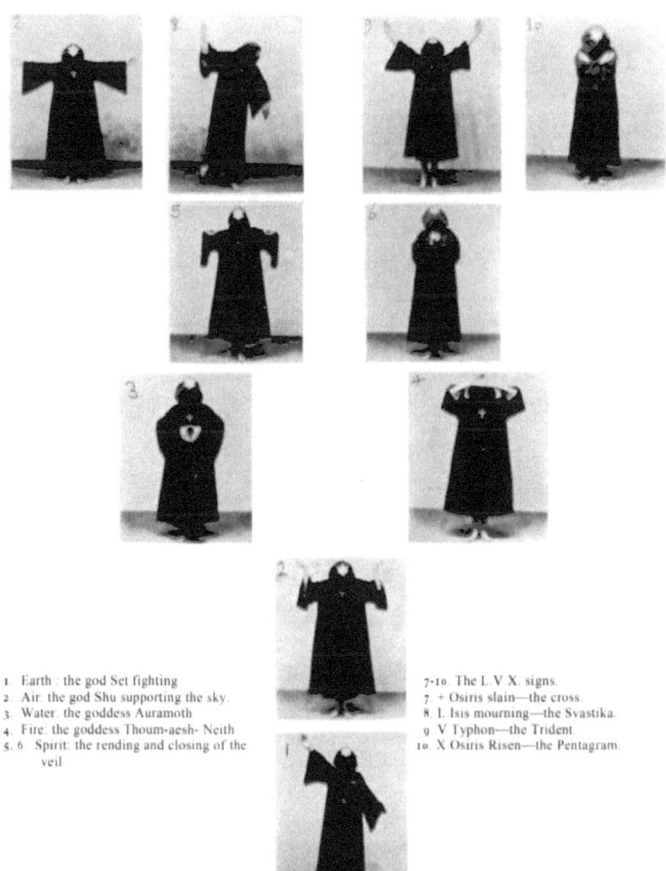

1. Earth : the god Set fighting
2. Air: the god Shu supporting the sky.
3. Water: the goddess Auramoth
4. Fire: the goddess Thoum-aesh- Neith
5. 6 Spirit: the rending and closing of the veil

7-10. The L.V.X. signs.
7. + Osiris slain—the cross
8. L. Isis mourning—the Svastika.
9. V Typhon—the Trident.
10. X Osiris Risen—the Pentagram.

The Signs of the Grades

IV

1. The Rituals of the Pentagram and Hexagram must be committed to memory. They are as follows.

THE LESSER RITUAL OF THE PENTAGRAM

(i) Touching the forehead, say Ateh (Unto Thee).

(ii) Touching the breast, say Malkuth (The Kingdom).

(iii) Touching the right shoulder, say ve-Geburah (and the Power).

(iv) Touching the left shoulder, say ve-Gedulah (and the Glory).

(v) Clasping the hands upon the breast, say le-Olahm, Amen (to the Ages, Amen).

(vi) Turning to the East, make a Pentagram (that of Earth) with the proper weapon (usually the Wand). Say (i.e., vibrate) I H V H.

(vii) Turning to the South, the same, but say A D N I.

(viii) Turning to the West, the same, but say A H I H.

(ix) Turning to the North, the same, but say A G L A.

Pronounce: Ye-ho-wau, Adonai, Eheieh, Agla.

(x) Extending the arms in the form of a Cross, say:

(xi) Before me Raphael;

(xii) Behind me Gabriel;

(xiii) On my right hand Michael;

(xiv) On my left hand Auriel;

(xv) For about me flames the Pentagram;

(xvi) And in the Column stands the six-rayed Star.

(xvii-xxi) Repeat (i) to (v), the "Qabalistic Cross."

THE GREATER RITUAL OF THE PENTAGRAM

The pentagrams are traced in the air with the sword or other weapon, the name spoken aloud, and the signs used, as illustrated.

VEL MANVS ET SAGITTÆ

The Greater Ritual of the Pentagram

The pentagrams are traced in the air with the sword or other weapon, the name spoken aloud, and the signs used, as illustrated.

THE PENTAGRAMS OF SPIRIT

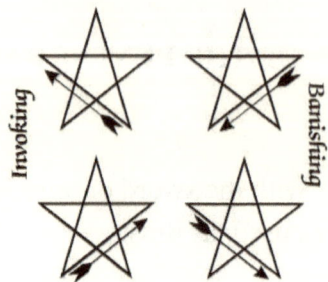

Equilibrium of Actives,
Name: A H I H (Eheieh).

Equilibrium of Passives,
Name: A G L A (Agla).

The signs of the Portal (*see* Illustrations): Extend the hands in front of you, palms outwards, separate them as if in the act of rending asunder a veil or curtain (actives), and then bring them together as if closing it up again and let them fall to the side (passives).[12]

(The Grade of the "Portal" is particularly attributed to the element of Spirit; it refers to the Sun; the paths of ⊡, ⊃, and ע are attributed to this degree. *See* "777," lines 6 and 31 bis.).

THE PENTAGRAMS OF FIRE

Name: A L H I M (Elohim).

The sign of 4°=7°: Raise the arms above the head and join the hands so that the tips of the fingers and of the thumbs meet, formulating a triangle. (*See* Illustration).

LIBER O

(The Grade of 4°=7° is particularly attributed to the element Fire; it refers to the planet Venus; the paths of ק, צ, and פ are attributed to this degree. For other attributions *see* "777," lines 7 and 31.).

THE PENTAGRAMS OF WATER

 Name: A L (El).

The sign of 3°=8°: Raise the arms till the elbows are on a level with the shoulders, bring the hands across the chest, touching the thumbs and tips of fingers so as to form a triangle apex downwards. (*See* Illustration).

(The Grade of 3°=8° is particularly attributed to the element of Water; it refers to the planet Mercury; the paths of ר and ש are attributed to this degree. For other attributions *see* "777," lines 8 and 23.).

THE PENTAGRAMS OF AIR

 Name: I H V H (Ye-ho-wau).

The sign of 2°=9°: Stretch both arms upwards and out-wards, the elbows bent at right-angles, the hands bent back, the palms upwards as if supporting a weight. (*See* Illustration).

(The Grade of 2°=9° is particularly attributed to the element Air; it refers to the Moon; the path of ת is attri-buted to this degree. For other attributions *see* "777," lines 9 and 11.).

The Pentagrams of Earth

Name: A D N I (Adonai).

The sign of 1°=10°: Advance the right foot, stretch out the right hand upwards and forwards, the left hand downwards and backwards, the palms open. (*See* Illustration).

(The Grade of 1°=10° is particularly attributed to the element of Earth. *See* "777," lines 10 and 32 bis.).

The Lesser Ritual of the Hexagram

This ritual is to be performed after the "Lesser Ritual of the Pentagram."

(i) Stand upright, feet together, left arm at side, right arm across body, holding the wand or other weapon upright in the median line. Then face East, and say:

(ii) I. N. R. I.
Yod. Nun. Resh. Yod.
Virgo, Isis, Mighty Mother.
Scorpio, Apophis, Destroyer.
Sol, Osiris, Slain and Risen.
Isis, Apophis, Osiris, IAO.

(iii) Extend the arms in the form of a cross, and say: "The sign of Osiris Slain." (*See* Illustration.)

(iv) Raise the right arm to point upwards, keeping the elbow square, and lower the left arm to point downwards, keeping the elbow square, while turning the head over the left shoulder looking down so that the eyes follow the left forearm, and say: "The sign of the Mourning of Isis." (*See* Illustration.)

THE PENTAGRAMS OF SPIRIT: Equilibrium of Actives, Name: A H I H (Eheieh). Equilibrium of Passives, Name: A G L A (Agla). The signs of the Portal: Extend the hands in front of you, palms outwards, separate them as if in the act of rending asunder a veil or curtain (actives), and then bring them together as if closing it up again and let them fall to the side (passives).

THE PENTAGRAMS OF FIRE: Name: A L H I M (Elohim). The sign of 4°=7°: Raise the arms above the head and join the hands so that the tips of the fingers and of the thumbs meet, formulating a triangle.

THE PENTAGRAMS OF WATER: Name: A L (El). The sign of 3°=8°: Raise the arms till the elbows are on a level with the shoulders, bring the hands across the chest, touching the thumbs and tips of fingers so as to form a triangle apex downwards.

THE PENTAGRAMS OF AIR: Name: I H V H (Ye-ho-wau). The sign of 2°=9°: Stretch both arms upwards and outwards, the elbows bent at right-angles, the hands bent back, the palms upwards as if supporting a weight.

THE PENTAGRAMS OF EARTH: Name: A D N I (Adonai). The sign of 1°=10°: Advance the right foot, stretch out the right hand upwards and forwards, the left hand downwards and backwards, the palms open.

THE LESSER RITUAL OF THE HEXAGRAM

This ritual is to be performed after the "Lesser Ritual of the Pentagram."

(v) Raise the arms at an angle of sixty degrees to each other above the head, which is thrown back, and say: "The sign of Apophis and Typhon." (*See* Illustration.)

(vi) Cross the arms on the breast, and bow the head, and say: "The sign of Osiris Risen." (*See* Illustration.)

(vii) Extend the arms again as in (iii) and cross them again as in (vi), saying: "L.V.X., Lux, the Light of the Cross."

(viii) With the magical weapon trace the Hexagram of Fire in the East, saying: "Ararita" (א ת י ר א ר א)

Which word consists of the initials of a sentence which means "One is His Beginning; One is His Individuality: His Permutation is One."

This hexagram consists of two equilateral triangles, both apices pointing upwards. Begin at the top of the upper triangle and trace it in a dextro-rotary direction. The top of the lower triangle should coincide with the central point of the upper triangle.

(ix) Trace the Hexagram of Earth in the South saying: "ARARITA."

This Hexagram has the apex of the lower triangle pointing downwards, and it should be capable of inscription in a circle.

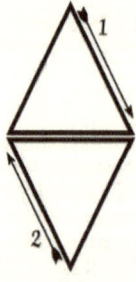

(x) Trace the Hexagram of Air in the West, saying: "ARARITA."

This hexagram is like that of Earth; but the bases of the triangles coincide, forming a diamond.

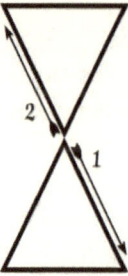

(xi) Trace the Hexagram of Water in the North, saying: "ARARITA."

This hexagram has the lower triangle placed above the upper, so that their apices coincide.

(xii) Repeat (i-vii)

The Banishing Ritual is identical, save that the direction of the Hexagrams must be reversed.[13]

(i) Stand upright, feet together, left arm at side, right arm across body, holding the wand or other weapon upright in the median line. Then face East, and say:

(ii) I. N. R. I. Yod. Nun. Resh. Yod. Virgo, Isis, Mighty Mother. Scorpio, Apophis, Destroyer. Sol, Osiris, Slain and Risen. Isis, Apophis, Osiris, IAO.

(iii) Extend the arms in the form of a cross, and say: "The sign of Osiris Slain."

(iv) Raise the right arm to point upwards, keeping the elbow square, and lower the left arm to point downwards, keeping the elbow square, while turning the head over the left shoulder looking down so that the eyes follow the left forearm, and say: "The sign of the Mourning of Isis."

(v) Raise the arms at an angle of sixty degrees to each other above the head, which is thrown back, and say: "The sign of Apophis and Typhon."

(vi) Cross the arms on the breast, and bow the head, and say: "The sign of Osiris Risen."

(vii) Extend the arms again as in (iii) and cross them again as in (vi), saying: "L.V.X., Lux, the Light of the Cross."

(viii) With the magical weapon trace the Hexagram of Fire in the East, saying: "Ararita" — which word consists of the initials of a sentence which means "One is His Beginning; One is His Individuality: His Permutation is One."

(ix) Trace the Hexagram of Earth in the South saying: "ARARITA."

(x) Trace the Hexagram of Air in the West, saying: "ARARITA."

(xi) Trace the Hexagram of Water in the North, saying: "ARARITA."

(xii) Repeat (i-vii). The Banishing Ritual is identical, save that the direction of the Hexagrams must be reversed.

THE GREATER RITUAL OF THE HEXAGRAM

To invoke or banish planets or zodiacal signs. The Hexagram of Earth alone is used. Draw the hexagram, beginning from the point which is attributed to the planet you are dealing with. (See "777," col. lxxxiii.) Thus to invoke Jupiter begin from the right-hand point of the lower triangle, dextro-rotary, and complete; then trace the upper triangle from its left-hand point and complete. Trace the astrological sigil of the planet in the centre of your hexagram. For the Zodiac use the hexagram of the planet which rules the sign you require; but draw the astrological sigil of the sign instead of that of the planet. For Caput and Cauda Draconis use the lunar hexagram, with the sigil thereof. To banish reverse the hexagram. In all cases use a conjuration first with Ararita, and next with the name of the God corresponding to the planet or sign you are dealing with.

The Greater Ritual of the Hexagram

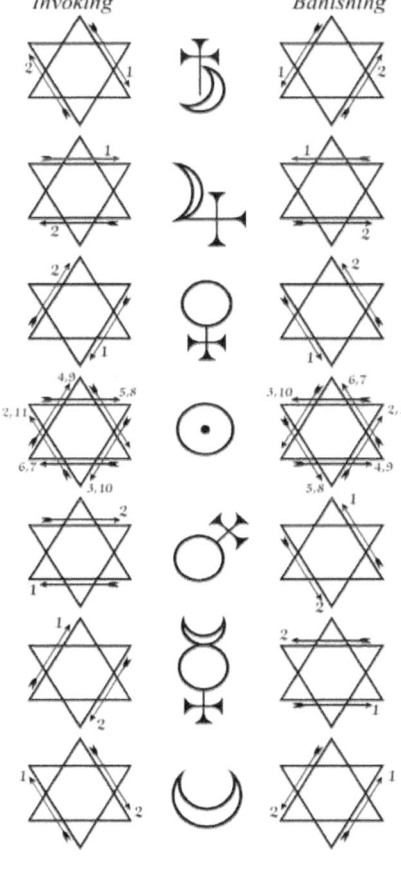

Invoking *Banishing*

To invoke or banish planets or zodiacal signs.

The Hexagram of Earth alone is used. Draw the hexagram, beginning from the point which is attributed to the planet you are dealing with. (See "777," col. lxxxiii.)

Thus to invoke Jupiter begin from the right-hand point of the lower triangle, dextro-rotary, and complete; then trace the upper triangle from its left-hand point and complete.

Trace the astrological sigil of the planet in the centre of your hexagram.

For the Zodiac use the hexagram of the planet which rules the sign you require ("777," col. cxxxviii.); but draw the astrological sigil of the sign instead of that of the planet.

The Greater Ritual of the Hexagram

2. These rituals should be practised until the figures drawn appear in flame, in flame so near to physical flame that it would perhaps be visible to the eyes of a bystander, were one present. It is alleged that some persons have attained the power of actually kindling fire by these means. Whether this be so or not, the power is not one to be aimed at.

3. Success in "banishing" is known by a "feeling of cleanliness" in the atmosphere; success in "invoking" by a "feeling of holiness." It is unfortunate that these terms are so vague. But at least make sure of this: that any imaginary figure or being shall instantly obey the will of the student, when he uses the appropriate figure. In obstinate cases, the form of the appropriate God may be assumed.

4. The banishing rituals should be used at the commencement of any ceremony whatever. Next, the student should use a general invocation, such as the "Preliminary Invocation" in the "Goetia," as well as a special invocation to suit the nature of his working.

5. Success in these verbal invocations is so subtle a matter, and its grades so delicately shaded, that it must be left to the good sense of the student to decide whether or not he should be satisfied with his result.

V

Viator in Regnis Arboris

1. Let the student be at rest in one of his prescribed positions, having bathed and robed with the proper decorum. Let the Place of Working be free from all disturbance, and let the preliminary purifications, banishings and invocations be duly accomplished, and, lastly, let the incense be kindled.

2. Let him imagine his own figure (preferably robed in the proper magical garments and armed with the proper magical weapons) as enveloping his physical body, or standing near to and in front of him.

3. Let him then transfer the seat of his consciousness to that imagined figure, so that it may seem to him that he is seeing with its eyes, and hearing with its ears. This will usually be the great difficulty of the operation.

4. Let him then cause that imagined figure to rise in the air to a great height above the earth.

5. Let him then stop and look about him. (It is sometimes difficult to open the eyes.)

6. Probably he will see figures approaching him, or become conscious of a landscape. Let him speak to such figures, and insist upon being answered, using the proper pentagrams and signs, as previously taught.

7. Let him travel about at will, either with or without guidance from such figure or figures.

8. Let him further employ such special invocations as will cause to appear the particular places he may wish to visit.

9. Let him beware of the thousand subtle attacks and deceptions that he will experience, carefully testing the truth of all with whom he speaks. Thus a hostile being may appear clothed with glory; the appropriate pentagrams will in such a case cause him to shrivel or decay.

10. Practice will make the student infinitely wary in these matters.

11. It is usually quite easy to return to the body; but should any difficulty arise, practice (again) will make the imagination fertile. For example, one may create in thought a chariot of fire with white horses, and command the charioteer to drive earthwards. It might be dangerous to go too far, or stay too long, for fatigue must be avoided. The danger spoken of is that of fainting, or of obsession, or loss of memory or other mental faculty.

12. Finally, let the student cause his imagined body in which he supposes himself to have been travelling to coincide with the physical, tightening his muscles, drawing in his breath, and putting his forefinger to his lips. Then let him "awake" by a well-defined act of will, and soberly and accurately record his experiences. It may be added that this apparently complicated experiment is perfectly easy to

perform. It is best to learn by "travelling" with a person already experienced in the matter. Two or three experiments should suffice to render the student confident and even expert.

VI

Sagitta trans Lunam

1. The previous experiment has little value, and leads to few results of importance. But it is susceptible of a development which merges into a form of Dharana—concentration—and as such may lead to the very highest ends. The principal use of the practice in the last chapter is to familiarise the student with every kind of obstacle and every kind of delusion, so that he may be perfect master of every idea that may arise in his brain, to dismiss it, to transmute it, to cause it instantly to obey his will.

2. Let him then begin exactly as before; but with the most intense solemnity and determination.

3. Let him be very careful to cause his imaginary body to rise in a line exactly perpendicular to the earth's tangent at the point where his physical body is situated (or, to put it more simply, straight upwards).

4. Instead of stopping, let him continue to rise until fatigue almost overcomes him. If he should find that he has stopped without willing to do so, and that figures appear, let him at all costs rise above them. Yea, though his very life tremble on his lips, let him force his way upward and onward!

5. Let him continue in this so long as the breath of life is in him. Whatever threatens, whatever allures, though it were Typhon and all his hosts loosed from the pit and leagued against him, though it were

from the very Throne of God Himself that a Voice issues bidding him stay and be content, let him struggle on, ever on.

6. At last there must come a moment when his whole being is swallowed up in fatigue, overwhelmed by its own inertia. Let him sink (when no longer can he strive, though his tongue be bitten through with the effort and the blood gush from his nostrils) into the blackness of unconsciousness; and then on coming to himself, let him write down soberly and accurately a record of all that hath occurred: yea, a record of all that hath occurred.

EXPLICIT

VI.
LIBER
RESH

VEL HELIOS

SVB FIGVRÂ CC

V

A∴A∴

Publication in Class D

Imprimatur:

N. Fra. A∴A∴

0. These are the adorations to be performed by all aspirants to the A∴A∴

1. Let him greet the Sun at dawn, facing East, giving the sign of his grade. And let him say in a loud voice:

> Hail unto Thee who art Ra in Thy rising, even unto Thee who art Ra in Thy strength, who travellest over the Heavens in Thy bark at the Uprising of the Sun.
>
> Tahuti standeth in His splendour at the prow, and Ra-Hoor abideth at the helm.
>
> Hail unto Thee from the Abodes of Night!

2. Also at Noon, let him greet the Sun, facing South, giving the sign of his grade. And let him say in a loud voice:

Hail unto Thee who art Ahathoor in Thy triumphing, even unto Thee who art Ahathoor in Thy beauty, who travellest over the Heavens in Thy bark at the Mid-course of the Sun.

Tahuti standeth in His splendour at the prow, and Ra-Hoor abideth at the helm.

Hail unto Thee from the Abodes of Morning!

3. Also, at Sunset, let him greet the Sun, facing West, giving the sign of his grade. And let him say in a loud voice:

Hail unto Thee who art Tum in Thy setting, even unto Thee who art Tum in Thy joy, who travellest over the Heavens in Thy bark at the Down-going of the Sun.

Tahuti standeth in His splendour at the prow, and Ra-Hoor abideth at the helm.

Hail unto Thee from the Abodes of Day!

4. Lastly, at Midnight, let him greet the Sun, facing North, giving the sign of his grade. And let him say in a loud voice:

Hail unto Thee who art Khephra in Thy hiding, even unto Thee who art Khephra in Thy silence, who travellest over the Heavens in Thy bark at the Midnight Hour of the Sun.

Tahuti standeth in His splendour at the prow, and Ra-Hoor abideth at the helm.

Hail unto Thee from the Abodes of Evening!

5. And after each of these invocations thou shalt give the sign of silence, and afterwards thou shalt perform the adoration that is taught thee by thy Superior. And then do thou compose thyself to holy meditation.

6. Also it is better if in these adorations thou assume the god-form of Whom thou adorest, as if thou didst unite with Him in the adoration of That which is beyond Him.

7. Thus shalt thou ever be mindful of the Great Work which thou hast undertaken to perform, and thus shalt thou be strengthened to pursue it unto the attainment of the Stone of the Wise, the Summum Bonum, True Wisdom and Perfect Happiness.

VII.

LIBER PORTA LUCIS

SVB FIGVRÂ X

V

A∴A∴

Publication in Class A

1. I behold a small dark orb, wheeling in an abyss of infinite space. It is minute among a myriad vast ones, dark amid a myriad bright ones.

2. I who comprehend in myself all the vast and the minute, all the bright and the dark, have mitigated the brilliance of mine unutterable splendour, sending forth V.V.V.V.V. as a ray of my light, as a messenger unto that small dark orb.

3. Then V.V.V.V.V. taketh up the word, and sayeth:

4. Men and women of the Earth, to you am I come from the Ages beyond the Ages, from the Space beyond your vision; and I bring to you these words.

5. But they heard him not, for they were not ready to receive them.

6. But certain men and women heard and understood, and through them shall this Knowledge be made known.

7. The least therefore of them, the servant of them all, writeth this book.

8. He writeth for those that are ready. Thus is it known if one be ready, if he be endowed with certain gifts, if he be fitted by birth, or by

wealth, or by intelligence, or by some other manifest sign. And the servants of the master by his insight shall judge of these.

9. This Knowledge is not for all men; few indeed are called, but of these few many are chosen.

10. This is the nature of the Work.

11. First, there are many and diverse conditions of life upon this earth. In all of these is some seed of sorrow. Who can escape from sickness and from old age and from death?

12. We are come to save our fellows from these things. For there is a life intense with knowledge and extreme bliss which is untouched by any of them.

13. To this life we attain even here and now. The adepts, the servants of V.V.V.V.V., have attained thereunto.

14. It is impossible to tell you of the splendours to which they have attained. Little by little, as your eyes grow stronger, will we unveil to you the ineffable glory of the Path of the Adepts, and its nameless goal.

15. Even as a man ascending a steep mountain is lost to sight of his friends in the valley, so must the adept seem. They shall say: He is lost in the clouds. But he shall rejoice in the sunlight above them, and come to the eternal snows.

16. Or as a scholar may learn some secret language of the ancients, his friends shall say: "Look! he pretends to read this book. But it is unintelligible—it is nonsense." Yet he delights in the Odyssey, while they read vain and vulgar things.

17. We shall bring you to Absolute Truth, Absolute Light, Absolute Bliss.

18. Many adepts throughout the ages have sought to do this; but their words have been perverted by their successors, and again and again the Veil has fallen upon the Holy of Holies.

19. To you who yet wander in the Court of the Profane we cannot reveal all; but you will easily understand that the religions of the world are but symbols and veils of the Absolute Truth. So also are the philosophies. To the adepts, seeing all things from above, there seems nothing to choose between Buddha and Mohammed, between Atheism and Theism.

20. The many change and pass; the one remains. Even as wood and coal and iron burn up together in one great flame, if only that furnace be of transcendent heat; so in the alembic of this spiritual alchemy, if only the zelator blow sufficiently upon his furnace, all the systems of earth are consumed in the One Knowledge.

21. Nevertheless, as a fire cannot be started with iron alone, in the beginning one system may be suited for one seeker, another for another.

22. We therefore who are without the chains of ignorance, look closely into the heart of the seeker and lead him by the path which is best suited to his nature unto the ultimate end of all things, the supreme realization, the Life which abideth in Light, yea, the Life which abideth in Light.

VIII.

LIBER TZADDI

VEL HAMVS

HERMETICVS SVB

FIGVRÂ XC

V

A∴A∴

Publication in Class A

0. In the name of the Lord of Initiation, Amen.

1. I fly and I alight as an hawk: of mother-of-emerald are my mighty-sweeping wings.

2. I swoop down upon the black earth; and it gladdens into green at my coming.

3. Children of Earth! rejoice! rejoice exceedingly; for your salvation is at hand.

4. The end of sorrow is come; I will ravish you away into mine unutterable joy.

5. I will kiss you, and bring you to the bridal; I will spread a feast before you in the house of happiness.

6. I am not come to rebuke you, or to enslave you.

7. I bid you not turn from your voluptuous ways, from your idleness, from your follies.

8. But I bring joy to your pleasure, peace to your languor, wisdom to your folly.

9. All that ye do is right, if so be that ye enjoy it.

10. I am come against sorrow, against weariness, against them that seek to enslave you.

11. I pour you lustral wine, that giveth you delight both at the sunset and the dawn.

12. Come with me, and I will give you all that is desirable upon the earth.

13. Because I give you that of which Earth and its joys are but as shadows.

14. They flee away, but my joy abideth even unto the end.

15. I have hidden myself beneath a mask: I am a black and terrible God.

16. With courage conquering fear shall ye approach me: ye shall lay down your heads upon mine altar, expecting the sweep of the sword.

17. But the first kiss of love shall be radiant on your lips; and all my darkness and terror shall turn to light and joy.

18. Only those who fear shall fail. Those who have bent their backs to the yoke of slavery until they can no longer stand upright; them will I despise.

19. But you who have defied the law; you who have conquered by subtlety or force; you will I take unto me, even I will take you unto me.

20. I ask you to sacrifice nothing at mine altar; I am the God who giveth all.

21. Light, Life, Love; Force, Fantasy, Fire; these do I bring you: mine hands are full of these.

22. There is joy in the setting-out; there is joy in the journey; there is joy in the goal.

23. Only if ye are sorrowful, or weary, or angry, or discomforted; then ye may know that ye have lost the golden thread, the thread wherewith I guide you to the heart of the groves of Eleusis.

24. My disciples are proud and beautiful; they are strong and swift; they rule their way like mighty conquerors.

25. The weak, the timid, the imperfect, the cowardly, the poor, the tearful—these are mine enemies, and I am come to destroy them.

26. This also is compassion: an end to the sickness of earth. A rooting-out of the weeds: a watering of the flowers.

27. O my children, ye are more beautiful than the flowers: ye must not fade in your season.

28. I love you; I would sprinkle you with the divine dew of immortality.

29. This immortality is no vain hope beyond the grave: I offer you the certain consciousness of bliss.

30. I offer it at once, on earth; before an hour hath struck upon the bell, ye shall be with Me in the Abodes that are beyond Decay.

31. Also I give you power earthly and joy earthly; wealth, and health, and length of days. Adoration and love shall cling to your feet, and twine around your heart.

32. Only your mouths shall drink of a delicious wine—the wine of Iacchus; they shall reach ever to the heavenly kiss of the Beautiful God.

33. I reveal unto you a great mystery. Ye stand between the abyss of height and the abyss of depth.

34. In either awaits a Companion; and the Companion is Yourself.

35. Ye can have no other Companion.

36. Many have arisen, being wise. They have said "Seek out the glittering Image in the place ever golden, and unite yourself with It."

37. Many have arisen, being foolish. They have said, "Stoop down unto the darkly splendid world, and be wedded to that Blind Creature of the Slime."

38. I who am beyond Wisdom and Folly, arise and say unto you: achieve both weddings! Unite yourself with both!

39. Beware, beware, I say, lest ye seek after the one and lose the other!

40. My adepts stand upright; their head above the heavens, their feet below the hells.

41. But since one is naturally attracted to the Angel, another to the Demon, let the first strengthen the lower link, the last attach more firmly to the higher.

42. Thus shall equilibrium become perfect. I will aid my disciples; as fast as they acquire this balanced power and joy so faster will I push them.

43. They shall in their turn speak from this Invisible Throne; their words shall illumine the worlds.

44. They shall be masters of majesty and might; they shall be beautiful and joyous; they shall be clothed with victory and splendour; they shall stand upon the firm foundation; the kingdom shall be theirs; yea, the kingdom shall be theirs.

In the name of the Lord of Initiation. Amen.

IX.

LIBER CL

A SANDAL

DE LEGE LIBELLꞶM

V

A∴A∴

Publication in Class E

PREFACE

THE LAW

Do what thou wilt shall be the whole of the Law.

IN RIGHTEOUSNESS OF HEART come hither, and listen: for it is I, ΤΟ ΜΕΓΑ ΘΗΡΙΟΝ, who gave this Law unto everyone that holdeth himself holy. It is I, not another, that willeth your whole Freedom, and the arising within you of full Knowledge and Power.

Behold! the Kingdom of God is within you, even as the Sun standeth eternal in the heavens, equal at midnight and at noon. He riseth not: he setteth not: it is but the shadow of the earth which concealeth him, or the clouds upon her face.

Let me then declare unto you the Mystery of this Law, as it hath been made known unto me in divers places, upon the mountains and in the deserts, but also in great cities, which thing I speak unto you for your comfort and good courage. And so be it unto all of you.

Know first, that from the Law spring four Rays or Emanations: so that if the Law be the centre of your own being, they must needs fill you with their secret goodness. And these four are Light, Life, Love, and Liberty.

By Light shall ye look upon yourselves, and behold All Things that are in Truth One Thing only, whose name hath been called No Thing for a cause which later shall be declared unto you. But the substance of Light is Life, since without Existence and Energy it were naught. By Life therefore are you made yourselves, eternal and incorruptible, flaming forth as suns, self-created and self-supported, each the sole centre of the Universe.

Now by the Light ye beheld, by Love ye feel. There is an ecstasy of pure Knowledge, and another of pure Love. And this Love is the force that uniteth things diverse, for the contemplation in Light of their Oneness. Know that the Universe is not at rest, but in extreme motion whose sum is Rest. And this understanding that Stability is Change, and Change Stability, that Being is Becoming, and Becoming Being, is the Key to the Golden Palace of this Law.

Lastly, by Liberty is the power to direct your course according to your Will. For the extent of the Universe is without bounds, and ye are free to make your pleasure as ye will, seeing that the diversity of being is infinite also. For this also is the Joy of the Law, that no two stars are alike, and ye must understand also that this Multiplicity is itself Unity, and without it Unity could not be. And this is an hard saying against Reason: ye shall comprehend, when, rising above Reason, which is but a manipulation of the Mind, ye come to pure Knowledge by direct perception of the Truth.

Know also that these four Emanations of the Law flame forth upon all paths: ye shall use them not only in these Highways of the Universe whereof I have written, but in every By-path of your daily life.

Love is the law, love under will.

I

OF LIBERTY

IT IS OF LIBERTY that I would first write unto you, for except ye be free to act, ye cannot act. Yet all four gifts of the Law must in some degree be exercised, seeing that these four are one. But for the Aspirant that cometh unto the Master, the first need is freedom.

The great bond of all bonds is ignorance. How shall a man be free to act if he know not his own purpose? You must therefore first of all discover which star of all the stars you are, your relation to the other stars about you, and your relation to, and identity with, the Whole.

In our Holy Books are given sundry means of making this discovery, and each must make it for himself, attaining absolute conviction by direct experience, not merely reasoning and calculating what is probable. And to each will come the knowledge of his finite will, whereby one is a poet, one prophet, one worker in steel, another in jade. But also to each the knowledge of his infinite Will, his destiny to perform the Great Work, the realization of his True Self. Of this Will let me therefore speak clearly unto all, since it pertaineth unto all.

Understand now that in yourselves is a certain discontent. Analyse well its nature: at the end is in every case one conclusion. The ill springs from the belief in two things, the Self and the Not-Self, and the conflict between them. This also is a restriction of the Will. He who is sick is in conflict with his own body: he who is poor is at odds with society: and so for the rest. Ultimately, therefore, the problem is how to destroy this perception of duality, to attain to the apprehension of unity.

Now then let us suppose that you have come to the Master, and that He has declared to you the Way of this attainment. What hindereth you? Alas! there is yet much Freedom afar off. Understand clearly this: that if you are sure of your Will, and sure of your means, then any thoughts or actions which are contrary to those means are contrary also to that Will.

If therefore the Master should enjoin upon you a Vow of Holy Obedience, compliance is not a surrender of the Will, but a fulfilment thereof. For see, what hindereth you? It is either from without or from within, or both. It may be easy for the strong-minded seeker to put his heel upon public opinion, or to tear from his heart the objects which he loves, in a sense: but there will always remain in himself many discordant affections, as also the bond of habit, and these also must he conquer. In our holiest Book it is written: "Thou hast no right but to do thy will. Do that, and no other shall say nay." Write it also in your heart and in your brain: for this is the key of the whole matter.

Here Nature herself be your preacher: for in every phenomenon of force and motion doth she proclaim aloud this truth. Even in so small a matter as driving a nail into a plank, hear this same sermon. Your nail must be hard, smooth, fine-pointed, or it will not move swiftly in the direction willed. Imagine then a nail of tinder-wood with twenty points —it is verily no longer a nail. Yet nigh all mankind are like unto this. They wish a dozen different careers; and the force which might have been sufficient to attain eminence in one is wasted on the others: they are null.

Here then let me make open confession, and say thus: though I pledged myself almost in boyhood to the Great Work, though to my aid came the most puissant forces in the Universe to hold me to it, though habit itself now constraineth me in the right direction, yet I have not fulfilled my Will: I turn aside daily from the appointed task. I waver. I falter. I lag.

Let this then be of great comfort to you all, that if I be so imperfect—and for very shame I have not emphasized that imperfection—if I, the chosen one, still fail, then how easy for yourselves to surpass me! Or, should you only equal me, then even so how great attainment should be yours!

Be of good cheer, therefore, since both my failure and my success are arguments of courage for yourselves.
Search yourselves cunningly, I pray you, analysing your inmost thoughts. And first you shall discard all those gross obvious hindrances to your Will: idleness, foolish friendships, waste employments or enjoyments.

Next, find the minimum of daily time which is in good sooth necessary to your natural life. The rest you shall devote to the True Means of your Attainment. And even these necessary hours you shall consecrate to the Great Work, saying consciously always while at these Tasks that you perform them only in order to preserve your body and mind in health for the right application to that sublime and single Object.

It shall not be very long before you come to understand that such a life is the true Liberty. You will feel distractions from your Will as what they are. They will no longer appear pleasant and attractive, but as bonds, as shames. And when you have attained this point, know that you have passed the Middle Gate of this Path. For you will have unified your Will.

Even thus, were a man sitting in a theatre where the play wearies him, he would welcome every distraction, and find amusement in any accident: but if he were intent upon the play, every such incident would annoy him. His attitude to these is then an indication of his attitude towards the play itself.

At first the habit of attention is hard to acquire. Persevere, and you will have spasms of revulsion periodically. Reason itself will attack you, saying: how can so strict a bondage be the Path of Freedom? Persevere. You have never yet known Liberty. When the temptations are overcome, the voice of Reason silenced, then will your soul bound forward unhampered upon its chosen course, and for the first time will you experience the extreme delight of being Master of Yourself, and therefore of the Universe.

When this is fully attained, when you sit securely in the saddle, then you may enjoy also all those distractions which first pleased you and then angered you. Now they will do neither any more: for they are your slaves and toys.

Until you have reached this point, you are not wholly free. You must kill out desire, and kill out fear. The end of all is the power to live according to your own nature, without danger that one part may develop to the detriment of the whole, or concern lest that danger should arise.

The sot drinks, and is drunken: the coward drinks not, and shivers: the wise man, brave and free, drinks, and gives glory to the Most High God.
This then is the Law of Liberty: you possess all Liberty in your own right, but you must buttress Right with Might: you must win Freedom for yourself in many a war. Woe unto the children who sleep in the Freedom that their forefathers won for them!

"There is no law beyond Do what thou wilt:" but it is only the greatest of the race who have the strength and courage to obey it.

O man! behold thyself! With what pains wast thou fashioned! What ages have gone to thy shaping! The history of the planet is woven into the very substance of thy brain! Was all this for naught? Is there no purpose in thee? Wast thou made thus that thou shouldst eat, and breed, and die? Think it not so! Thou dost incorporate so many elements, thou art the fruit of so many aeons of labour, thou art fashioned thus as thou art, and not otherwise, for some colossal End. Nerve thyself, then, to seek it and to do it. Naught can satisfy thee but the fulfilment of thy transcendent Will, that is hidden within thee. For this, then, up to arms! Win thine own Freedom for thyself! Strike hard!

II

OF LOVE

IT IS WRITTEN THAT "Love is the law, love under will." Herein is an Arcanum concealed, for in the Greek Language Αγαπη, Love, is of the same numerical value as Θελημα, Will. By this we understand that the Universal Will is of the nature of Love.

Now Love is the enkindling in ecstasy of Two that will to become One. It is thus an Universal formula of High Magick. For see now how all things, being in sorrow caused by dividuality, must of necessity will Oneness as their medicine.

Here also is Nature monitor to them that seek Wisdom at her breast: for in the uniting of elements to opposite polarities is there a glory of heat, of light, and of electricity. Thus also in mankind do we behold the spiritual fruit of poetry and all genius, arising from the seed of what is but an animal gesture, in the estimation of such as are schooled in Philosophy. And it is to be noted strongly that the most violent and divine passions are those between people of utterly unharmonious natures.

But now I would have you know that in the mind are no such limitations in respect of species as prevent a man falling in love with an inanimate object, or an idea. For to him that is in any wise advanced upon the Way of Meditation it appears that all objects save the One Object are distasteful, even as appeared formerly in respect of his chance wishes to the Will.

So therefore all objects must be grasped with the mind, and heated in the sevenfold furnace of Love, until with explosion of ecstasy they unite, and disappear, for they, being imperfect, are destroyed utterly in the creation of the Perfection of Union, even as the persons of the Lover and the Beloved are fused into the spiritual gold of Love, which knoweth no person, but comprehendeth all.

Yet since each star is but one star, and the coming together of any two is but one partial rapture, so must the aspirant to our holy Science and Art increase constantly by this method of assimilating ideas, that in the end, become capable of apprehending the Universe in one thought, he may leap forth upon It with the massed violence of his Self, and destroying both these, become that Unity whose name is No Thing.

Seek ye all therefore constantly to unite yourselves in rapture with each and every thing that is, and that by utmost passion and lust of Union. To this end take chiefly all such things as are naturally repulsive. For what is pleasant is assimilated easily and without ecstasy: it is in the transfiguration of the loathsome and abhorred into The Beloved that the Self is shaken to the root in Love.

Thus in human love also we see that mediocrities among men mate with null women: but History teacheth us that the supreme masters of the world seek ever the vilest and most horrible creatures for their concubines, overstepping even the limiting laws of sex and species in their necessity to transcend normality. It is not enough in such natures to excite lust or passion: the imagination itself must be inflamed by every means.

For us, then, emancipated from all base law, what shall we do to satisfy our Will to Unity? No less a mistress than the Universe: no lupanar more cramped than Infinite Space: no night of rape that is not coeval with Eternity!

Consider that as Love is mighty to bring forth all Ecstasy, so absence of Love is the greatest craving. Whoso is balked in Love suffereth indeed, but he that hath not actively that passion in his heart towards some object is weary with the ache of craving. And this state is called mystically "Dryness." For this there is, as I believe, no cure but patient persistence in a Rule of Life.

But this Dryness hath its virtue, in that thereby the soul is purged of those things that impeach the Will: for when the drouth is altogether perfect, then it is certain that by no means can the Soul be satisfied, save by the Accomplishment of the Great Work. And this is in strong souls a stimulus to the Will. It is the Furnace of Thirst that burneth up all dross within us.But to each act of Will is a particular Dryness corresponding: and as Love increaseth within you, so does the torment of His absence. Be this also unto you for a consolation in the ordeal! Moreover, the more fierce the plague of impotence, the more swiftly and suddenly is it wont to abate.

Here is the method of Love in Meditation. Let the Aspirant first practice and then discipline himself in the Art of fixing the attention on any thing whatsoever at will, without permitting the least imaginable distraction. Let him also practice the art of the Analysis of Ideas, and that of refusing to allow the mind its natural reaction to them, pleasant or unpleasant, thus fixing himself in Simplicity and Indifference.

These things being achieved in their ripe season, be it known to you that all ideas will have become equal to your apprehension, since each is simple and each indifferent: any one of them remaining in the mind at Will without stirring or striving, or tending to pass on to any other. But each idea will possess one special quality common to all: this, that no one of any of them is The Self, inasmuch as it is perceived by The Self as Something Opposite.

When this is thorough and profound in the impact of its realization, then is the moment for the aspirant to direct his Will to Love upon it, so that his whole consciousness findeth focus upon that One Idea. And at the first it may be fixed and dead, or lightly held. This may then pass into dryness, or into repulsion. Then at last by pure persistence in that Act of Will to Love, shall Love himself arise, as a bird, as a flame, as a song, and the whole Soul shall wing a fiery path of music unto the Ultimate Heaven of Possession.

Now in this method there are many roads and ways, some simple and direct, some hidden and mysterious, even as it is with human love whereof no man hath made so much as the first sketches for a Map: for Love is infinite in diversity even as are the Stars. For this cause do I leave Love himself master in the heart of every one of you: for he shall teach you rightly if you but serve him with diligence and devotion even to abandonment.

Nor shall you take umbrage at the strange pranks that he shall play: for He is a wayward boy and wanton, wise in the Wiles of Aphrodite Our Lady His sweet Mother: and all His jests and cruelties are spices in a confection cunning as no art may match.

Rejoice therefore in all His play, not remitting in any wise your own ardour, but glowing with the sting of His whips, and making of Laughter itself a sacrament adjuvant to Love, even as in the Wine of Rheims is sparkle and bite, like as they were ministers to the High Priest of Intoxication.

It is also fit that I write to you of the importance of Purity in Love. Now this matter concerneth not in any wise the object or the method of the practice: the one thing essential is that no alien element should intrude. And this is of most particular pertinence to the aspirant in that primary and mundane aspect of his work wherein he establisheth himself in the method through his natural affections.
For know, that all things are masks or symbols of the One Truth, and nature serveth alway to point out the higher perfection under the veil

of the lower perfection. So then all the Art and Craft of human love shall serve you as an hieroglyphic: for it is written that That which is above is like that which is below: and That which is below is like that which is above.

Therefore also doth it behoove you to take well heed lest in any manner you fail in this business of purity. For though each act is to be complete on its own plane, and no influence of any other plane is to be brought in for interference or admixture, for that such is all impurity, yet each act should in itself be so complete and perfect that it is a mirror of the perfection of every plane, and thereby becometh partaker of the pure Light of the highest. Also, since all acts are to be acts of Will in Freedom on every plane, all planes are in reality but one: and thus the lowest expression of any function of that Will is to be at the same time an expression of the highest Will, or only true Will, which is that already implied in the acceptance of the Law.

Be it also well understood that it is not necessary or right to shut off natural activity of any kind, as certain false folk, eunuchs of the spirit, most foully teach, to the destruction of many. For in every thing soever inhereth its own perfection proper to it, and to neglect the full operation and function of any one part bringeth distortion and degeneration to the whole. Act therefore in all ways, but transforming the effect of all these ways to the One Way of the Will. And this is possible, because all ways are in actual Truth One Way, the Universe being itself One and One Only, and its appearance as Multiplicity that cardinal illusion which it is the very object of Love to dissipate.

In the achievement of Love are two principles, that of mastering, and that of yielding. But the nature of these is hard to explain, for they are subtle, and are best taught by Love Himself in the course of the Operations. But it is to be said generally that the choice of one formula or the other is automatic, being the work of that inmost Will which is alive within you. Seek not then to determine consciously this decision, for herein true instinct is not liable to err.

But now I end, without further words: for in our Holy Books are written many details of the actual practices of Love. And those are the best and truest which are most subtly written in symbol and image, especially in Tragedy and Comedy, for the whole nature of these things is in this kind, Life itself being but the fruit of the flower of Love.

It is then of Life that I must needs now write to you, seeing that by every act of Will in Love you are creating it, a quintessence more mysterious and joyous than you deem, for this which men call life is but a shadow of that true Life, your birthright, and the gift of the Law of Thelema.

III

OF LIFE

SYSTOLE AND DIASTOLE: these are the phases of all component things. Of such also is the life of man. Its curve arises from the latency of the fertilized ovum, say you, to a zenith whence it declines to the nullity of death? Rightly considered, this is not wholly truth. The life of man is but one segment of a serpentine curve which reaches out to infinity, and its zeros but mark the changes from the plus to minus, and minus to plus, coefficients of its equation. It is for this cause, among many others, that wise men in old time chose the Serpent as the Hieroglyph of Life.

Life then is indestructible as all else is. All destruction and construction are changes in the nature of Love, as I have written to you in the former chapter proximate. Yet even as the blood in one pulse-throb of the wrist is not the same blood as that in the next, so individuality is in part destroyed as each life passeth; nay, even with every thought.

What then maketh man, if he dieth and is reborn a changeling with each breath? This: the consciousness of continuity given by memory, the conception of his Self as something whose existence, far from being threatened by these changes, is in verity assured by them. Let then the aspirant to the sacred Wisdom consider his Self no more as one segment of the Serpent, but as the whole. Let him extend his consciousness to regard both birth and death as incidents trivial as systole and diastole of the heart itself, and necessary as they to its function.

To fix the mind in this apprehension of Life, two modes are preferred, as preliminary to the greater realizations. The first mode is the acquisition of the Magical Memory so-called, and the means is described with accuracy and clearness in certain of our Holy Books. But for nearly all men this is found to be a practice of exceeding difficulty. Let then the aspirant follow the impulse of his own Will in the decision to choose this or no.

The second mode is easy, agreeable, not tedious, and in the end as certain as the other. But as the way of error in the former lieth in Discouragement, so in the latter are you to be ware of False Paths. This second mode is to dissociate the beings which make up your life.

Firstly, because it is easiest, you should segregate that Form which is called the Body of Light (and also by many other names) and set yourself to travel in this Form, making systematic exploration of those worlds which are to other material things what your own Body of Light is to your own material form.

Now it will occur to you in these travels that you come to many Gates which you are not able to pass. This is because your Body of Light is itself as yet not strong enough, or subtle enough, or pure enough: and you must then learn to dissociate the elements of that body by a process similar to the first, your consciousness remaining in the higher and leaving the lower.

In this practice do you continue, bending your Will like a great Bow to drive the Arrow of your consciousness through heavens ever higher and holier. But the continuance in this Way is itself of vital value: for it shall be that presently habit herself shall persuade you that the body which is born and dieth within so little a space as one cycle of Neptune in the Zodiac is no essential of your Self, that the Life of which you are become partaker, while itself subject to the Law of action and reaction, ebb and flow, systole and diastole, is yet insensible to the afflictions of that life which you formerly held to be your sole bond with existence.

And here must you resolve your Self to make the mightiest endeavours: for so flowered are the meadows of this Eden, and so sweet the fruit of its orchards, that you will love to linger among them, and to take delight in sloth and dalliance therein. Therefore I write to you with energy that these enjoyments are dependent upon duality, so that their true name is Sorrow of Illusion, like that of the normal life of man, which you have set out to transcend.

Be it according to your Will, but learn this, that (as it is written) they only are happy who have desired the unattainable. It is then best, ultimately, if it be your Will to find alway your chiefest pleasure in Love, that is, in Conquest, and in Death, that is, in Surrender, as I have written to you already. Thus then you shall delight in these delights aforesaid, but only as toys, holding your manhood firm and keen to pierce to deeper and holier ecstasies without arrest of Will.

Furthermore, I would have you to know that in this practice, pursued with ardour unquenchable, is this especial grace, that you will come as it were by fortune into states which transcend the practice itself, being of the nature of those works of Pure Light of which I will write to you in the chapter following after this. For there be certain Gates which no being who is still conscious of dividuality, that is, of the Self and not-Self as opposites, may pass through: and in the storming of those Gates by fiery assault of lust celestial, your flame will burn vehemently against your gross Self, though it be already divine beyond your present imagining, and devour it in a mystical death, so that in the Passing of the Gate all is dissolved in formless Light of Unity.

Now then, returning from these states of being, and in the return also there is a Mystery of Joy, you will be weaned from the Milk of Darkness of the Moon, and made partaker of the Sacrament of Wine that is the blood of the Sun. Yet at the first there may be shock and conflict, for the old thought persists by force of its habit: it is for you to create by repeated act the true right habit of this consciousness of the Life which abideth in Light.

And this is easy, if your will be strong: for the true Life is so much more vivid and quintessential than the false that (as I rudely estimate) one hour of the former makes an impression on the memory equal to one year of the latter. One single experience, in duration it may be but a few seconds of terrestrial time, is sufficient to destroy the belief in the reality of our vain life on earth: but this wears gradually away if the consciousness, through shock or fear, adhere not to it, and the Will strive not continually to repetition of that bliss, more beautiful and terrible than death, which it hath won by virtue of Love.

There be moreover many other modes of attaining the apprehension of true Life, and these two following are of much value in breaking up the ice of your mortal error in the vision of your being. And of these the first is the constant contemplation of the Identity of Love and Death, and the understanding of the dissolution of the body as an Act of Love done upon the Body of the Universe, as also it is written at length in our Holy Books. And with this goeth, as it were sister with twin brother, the practice of mortal love as a sacrament symbolical of that great Death: as it is written "Kill thyself" and again "Die daily." And the second of these lesser modes is the practice of the mental apprehension and analysis of ideas, mainly as I have already taught you, but with especial emphasis in choice of things naturally repulsive, in particular death itself, and its phenomena ancillary. Thus the Buddha bade his disciples to meditate upon Ten Impurities, that is, upon ten cases of death or decomposition, so that the Aspirant, identifying himself with his own corpse in all these imagined forms, might lose the natural horror, loathing, fear or disgust which he might have had for them. Know this, that every idea of every sort becomes unreal, phantastic, and most manifest illusion, if it be subjected to persistent investigation, with concentration. And this is particularly easy to attain in the case of all bodily impressions, because all material things, and especially those of which we are first conscious, namely, our own bodies, are the grossest and most unnatural of all falsities. For there is in us all, latent, that Light wherein no error may endure, and It already teaches our instinct to reject first of all those veils which are most closely wrapt about It. Thus also in meditation it is (for many men) most profitable to concentrate the Will to Love upon the sacred centres of nervous force: for they, like all things, are apt images or true reflexions of their semblances in finer spheres: so that, their gross images being dissipated by the dissolving acid of the Meditation, their finer souls appear (so to speak) naked, and display their force and glory in the consciousness of the aspirant.

Yea, verily, let your Will to Love burn eagerly toward this creation in yourselves of the true Life that rolls its waves across the shoreless sea of Time! Live not your petty lives in fear of the hours! The Moon and Sun and Stars by which ye measure Time are themselves but servants of that Life which pulses in you, joyous drum-beat as you march triumphant through the Avenue of the Ages. Then, when each birth and death of yours are recognized in this perception as mere milestones on your ever-living Road, what of the foolish incidents of your mean lives?

Are they not grains of sand blown by the desert wind, or pebbles that you spurn with your winged feet, or grassy hollows where you press the yielding and elastic turf and moss with lyrical dances? To him who lives in Life naught matters: his is eternal motion, energy, delight of never-failing Change: unwearied, you pass on from aeon to aeon, from star to star, the Universe your playground, its infinite variety of sport ever old and ever new. All those ideas which bred sorrow and fear are known in their truth, and thus become the seed of joy: for you are certain beyond all proof that you can never die: that though you change, change is part of your own nature: the Great Enemy is become the Great Ally.

And now, rooted in this perfection, your Self become the very Tree of Life, you have a fulcrum for your lever: you are ready to understand that this pulsation of Unity is itself Duality, and therefore, in the highest and most sacred sense, still Sorrow and Illusion; which, having comprehended, aspire yet again, even unto the Fourth of the Gifts of the Law, unto the End of the Path, even unto Light.

IV

OF LIGHT

I PRAY YOU, be patient with me in that which I shall write concerning Light: for here is a difficulty, ever increasing, in the use of words. Moreover, I am myself carried away constantly and overwhelmed by the sublimity of this matter, so that plain speech may whirl into lyric, when I would plod peaceably with didactic, expression.

My best hope is that you may understand by virtue of the sympathy of your intuition, even as two lovers may converse in language as unintelligible to others as it seemeth silly, wanton, and dull. So may I that am inflamed with love of this Light, and drunken on the wine Ethereal of this Light, communicate not so much with your reason and intelligence, but with that principle hidden in yourself which is ready to partake with me.

In exercise of Will and Love are implied motion and change, but in Life is gained an Unity which moveth and changeth only in pulse or in phase, and is even as music. Yet in the attainment of this Life you will already have experienced that the Quintessence thereof is pure Light, an ecstasy formless, and without bound or mark. In this Light naught exists, for It is homogeneous: and therefore have men called it Silence, and Darkness, and Nothing. But in this, as in all other effort to name it, is the root of every falsity and misapprehension, since all words imply some duality. Therefore, though I call it Light, it is not Light, nor absence of Light.

Many also have sought to describe it by contradiction, since through transcendent negation of all speech it may by some natures be attained. Also by images and symbols have men striven to express it: but always in vain. Yet those that were ready to apprehend the nature of this Light have understood by sympathy: and so shall it be with you who read this little book, loving it.

For this Universe is in Truth Zero, being an equation whereof Zero is the sum. Whereof this is the proof, that if not, it would be unbalanced, and something would have come from Nothing, which is absurd. This Light or Nothing is then the Resultant or Totality thereof in pure Perfection; and all other states, positive or negative, are imperfect, since they omit their opposites.

Yet, I would have you consider that this equality or identity of equation between all things and No thing is most absolute, so that you will remain no more in one than you did in the other. And you will understand this greatest Mystery very easily in the light of those other experiences which you have enjoyed, wherein motion and rest, change and stability, and many other subtle opposites, have been redeemed to identity by the force of your holy meditation.

The greatest gift of the Law, then, cometh forth by the most perfect practice of the Three Lesser Gifts. And so thoroughly must you travail in this Work that you are able to pass from one side of the equation to the other at will: nay, to comprehend the whole at once, and for ever. Thus then your time-and-space-bound soul shall travel according to its nature in its orbit, revealing the Law to them that walk in chains, for that this is your particular function.

I wish to write to you with regard to the number 93, the number of Θελημα. For it is not only the number of its interpretation Αγαπη, but also that of a Word unknown to you unless you be Neophyte of our Holy Order of the A∴A∴ which word representeth in itself the arising of the Speech from the Silence, and the return thereunto in the End. Now the number 93 is thrice 31, which is in Hebrew LA, that is to say NOT, and so it denieth extension in the three dimensions of Space. Also I would have you to meditate closely upon the name NU that is 56, which we are told to divide, add, multiply, and understand. By division cometh forth 0.12, as if it were written Nuith! Hadith! Ra-Hoor-Khuith! before the Dyad. By addition ariseth Eleven, the number of True Magick: and by multiplication Three Hundred, the Number of the Holy Spirit or Fire, the letter Shin, wherein all things are consumed utterly. With these considerations, and a full understanding of the mysteries of the Number 666 and 418, you will be armed mightily in this Way of far flight. But you should also consider all numbers in their scales. For there is no means of resolution better than this of pure mathematics, since already therein are gross ideas made fine, and all is ordered and ready for the Alchemy of the Great Work.

I have already written to you of how, in the Will of Love, Light ariseth as the secret part of Life. And in the first, the little, Loves, the attained Life is still personal: later, it becometh impersonal and universal. Now then is Will arrived, may I say so, at its magnetic pole, whence the lines of force point alike every way and no way: and Love also is no more a work, but a state. These qualities are become part of the Universal Life, which proceedeth infinitely with the enjoyment of the Will, and of Love as inherent therein.

These things therefore, in their perfection, have lost their names, and their natures. Yet these were the Substance of Life, its Father and Mother: and without their operation and impact Life itself will gradually cease its pulsations. But since the infinite energy of the whole Universe is therein, what then is possible but that it return to its own First Intention, dissolving itself little by little into that Light which is its most secret and most subtle Nature?

Now here is the Mystery of the Origin of Evil. Firstly, by Evil we mean that which is in opposition to our own wills: it is therefore a relative, and not an absolute, term. For everything which is the greatest evil of some one is the greatest good of some other, just as the hardness of the wood which wearieth the axeman is the safety of him that ventureth himself upon the sea in a ship built of that wood. And this is a truth easy to apprehend, being superficial, and intelligible to the common mind.

All evil is thus relative, or apparent, or illusory: but, returning to philosophy, I will repeat that its root is always in duality. Therefore the escape from this apparent evil is to seek the Unity, which you shall do as I have already shewn you. But I will make mention of that which is written concerning this in The Book of the Law.
The first step being Will, Evil appears as by this definition, "all that hinders the execution of the Will." Therefore is it written: "The word of Sin is Restriction." It should also be noted that in The Book of the Thirty Aethyrs Evil appears as Choronzon whose number is 333, which in Greek importeth Impotence and Idleness: and the nature of Choronzon is Dispersion and Incoherence.

Then in the Way of Love Evil appears as "all that which tends to prevent the Union of any two things." Thus The Book of the Law sayeth, under the figure of the Voice of Nuit: "take your fill and will of love as ye will, when, where, and with whom ye will! But always unto me." For every act of Love must be "under will," that is, in accordance with the True Will, which is not to rest content with things partial and transitory, but to proceed firmly to the End. So also, in The Book of the Thirty Aethyrs, the Black Brothers are those who shut themselves up, unwilling to destroy themselves by Love.

Thirdly, in the Way of Life Evil appears under a subtler form as "all that which is not impersonal and universal." Here The Book of the

Law, by the Voice of Hadit, informeth us: "In the sphere I am everywhere the centre..." And again: "I am Life and the giver of Life... 'Come unto me' is a foolish word: for it is I that go.... For I am perfect, being Not." For this Life is in every place and time at once, so that in It these limitations no longer exist. And you will have seen this for yourself, that in every act of Love time and space disappear with the creation of the Life by its virtue, as doth also personality itself. For the third time, then, in even subtler sense, "The word of Sin is Restriction."

Lastly, in the Way of Light this same versicle is the key to the conception of Evil. But here Restriction is in the failure to solve the Great Equation, and, later, to prefer one expression or phase of the Universe to another. Against this we are warned in The Book of the Law by the Word of Nuit, saying: "None... and two. For I am divided for love's sake, for the chance of union," and therefore, "If this be not aright: if ye confound the space marks, saying, They are many... then expect the direful judgements..."

Now therefore by the favour of Thoth am I come to the end of this my book: and do you arm yourselves accordingly with the Four Weapons: the Wand for Liberty, the Cup for Love, the Sword for Life, the Disk for Light: and with these work all wonders by the Art of High Magick under the Law of the New Aeon, whose Word is Θελημα.

X.

LIBER LXV

LIBER CORDIS CINCTI SERPENTE
SUB FIGURÂ ADNI

V

A∴A∴

Publication in Class A

I

*I am the Heart; and the Snake is entwined About
the invisible core of the mind.
Rise, O my snake! It is now is the hour
Of the hooded and holy ineffable flower.
Rise, O my snake, into brilliance of bloom
On the corpse of Osiris afloat in the tomb!
O heart of my mother, my sister, mine own,
Thou art given to Nile, to the terror Typhon! Ah
me! but the glory of ravening storm Enswathes
thee and wraps thee in frenzy of form. Be still, O
my soul! that the spell may dissolve As the
wands are upraised and the æons revolve.
Behold! in my beauty how joyous thou art,
O Snake that caresses the crown of mine heart!
Behold! we are one, and the tempest of years
Goes down to the dusk, and the Beetle appears.*

O Beetle! the drone of Thy dolorous note
Be ever the trance of this tremulous throat!
I await the awakening! The summons on high
From the Lord Adonai, from the Lord Adonai!

2. Adonai spake unto V.V.V.V.V., saying: There must ever be division in the word.

3. For the colours are many, but the light is one.

4. Therefore thou writest that which is of mother of emerald, and of lapis-lazuli, and of turquoise, and of alexandrite.

5. Another writeth the words of topaz, and of deep amethyst, and of gray sapphire, and of deep sapphire with a tinge as of blood.

6. Therefore do ye fret yourselves because of this.

7. Be not contented with the image.

8. I who am the Image of an Image say this.

9. Debate not of the image, saying Beyond! Beyond! One mounteth unto the Crown by the moon and by the Sun, and by the arrow, and by the Foundation, and by the dark home of the stars from the black earth.

10. Not otherwise may ye reach unto the Smooth Point.

11. Nor is it fitting for the cobbler to prate of the Royal matter. O cobbler! mend me this shoe, that I may walk. O king! if I be thy son, let us speak of the Embassy to the King thy Brother.

12. Then was there silence. Speech had done with us awhile. There is a light so strenuous that it is not perceived as light.

13. Wolf's bane is not so sharp as steel; yet it pierceth the body more subtly.

14. Even as evil kisses corrupt the blood, so do my words devour the spirit of man.

15. I breathe, and there is infinite dis-ease in the spirit.

16. As an acid eats into steel, as a cancer that utterly corrupts the body; so am I unto the spirit of man.

17. I shall not rest until I have devoured it all.

18. So also the light that is absorbed. One absorbs little, and is called white and glistening; one absorbs all and is called black.

19. Therefore, O my darling, art thou black.

20. O my beautiful, I have likened thee to a jet Nubian slave, a boy of melancholy eyes.

21. O the filthy one! the dog! they cry against thee. Because thou art my beloved.

22. Happy are they that praise thee; for they see thee with Mine eyes.

23. Not aloud shall they praise thee; but in the night watch one shall steal close, and grip thee with the secret grip; another shall privily cast a crown of violets over thee; a third shall greatly dare, and press mad lips to thine.

24. Yea! the night shall cover all, the night shall cover all.

25. Thou wast long seeking Me; thou didst run forward so fast that I was unable to come up with thee. O thou darling fool! what bitterness thou didst crown thy days withal.

26. Now I am with thee; I will never leave thy being.

27. For I am the soft sinuous one entwined about thee, heart of gold!

28. My head is jewelled with twelve stars. My body is white as milk of the stars; it is bright with the blue of the abyss of stars invisible.

29. I have found that which could not be found; I have found a vessel of quicksilver.

30. Thou shalt instruct thy servant in his ways, thou shalt speak often with him.

31. (The scribe looketh upwards and crieth) Amen! Thou hast spoken it, Lord God!

32. Further Adonai spake unto V.V.V.V.V. and said:

33. Let us take our delight in the multitude of men! Let us shape unto ourselves a boat of mother-of-pearl from them, that we may ride upon the river of Amrit!

34. Thou seest yon petal of amaranth, blown by the wind from the low sweet brows of Hathor?

35. (The Magister saw it and rejoiced in the beauty of it.) Listen!

36. (From a certain world came an infinite wail.) That falling petal seemed to the little ones a wave to engulf their continent.

37. So they will reproach thy servant, saying: Who hath set thee to save us?

38. He will be sore distressed.

39. All they understand not that thou and I are fashioning a boat of mother-of-pearl. We will sail down the river of Amrit even to the yew-groves of Yama, where we may rejoice exceedingly.

40. The joy of men shall be our silver gleam, their woe our blue gleam—all in the mother-of-pearl.

41. (The scribe was wroth thereat. He spake: O Adonai and my master, I have borne the inkhorn and pen without pay, in order that I might search this river of Amrit, and sail thereon as one of ye. This I demand for my fee, that I partake of the echo of your kisses.)

42. (And immediately it was granted unto him.)

43. (Nay; but not therewith was he content. By an infinite abasement unto shame did he strive. Then a voice:)

44. Thou strivest ever; even in thy yielding thou strivest to yield—and lo! thou yieldest not.

45. Go thou unto the outermost places and subdue all things.

46. Subdue thy fear and thy disgust. Then—yield!

47. There was a maiden that strayed among the corn, and sighed; then grew a new birth, a narcissus, and therein she forgot her sighing and her loneliness.

48. Even instantly rode Hades heavily upon her, and ravished her away.

49. (Then the scribe knew the narcissus in his heart; but because it came not to his lips, therefore was he shamed and spake no more.)

50. Adonai spake yet again with V.V.V.V.V. and said: The earth is ripe for vintage; let us eat of her grapes and be drunken thereon.

51. And V.V.V.V.V. answered and said: O my lord, my dove, my excellent one, how shall this word seem unto the children of men?

52. And He answered him: Not as thou canst see. It is certain that every letter of this cipher hath some value; but who shall determine the value? For it varieth ever, according to the subtlety of Him that made it.

53. And He answered Him: Have I not the key thereof? I am clothed with the body of flesh; I am one with the Eternal and Omnipotent God.

54. Then said Adonai: Thou hast the Head of the Hawk, and thy Phallus is the Phallus of Asar. Thou knowest the white, and thou knowest the black, and thou knowest that these are one. But why seekest thou the knowledge of their equivalence?

55. And he said: That my Work may be right.

56. And Adonai said: The strong brown reaper swept his swathe and rejoiced. The wise man counted his muscles, and pondered, and understood not, and was sad. Reap thou, and rejoice!

57. Then was the Adept glad, and lifted his arm. Lo! an earthquake, and plague, and terror on the earth! A casting down of them that sate in high places; a famine upon the multitude.

58. And the grape fell ripe and rich into his mouth.

59. Stained is the purple of thy mouth, O brilliant one, with the white glory of the lips of Adonai.

60. The foam of the grape is like the storm upon the sea; the ships tremble and shudder, the shipmaster is afraid.

61. That is thy drunkenness, O holy one, and the winds whirl away the soul of the scribe into the happy haven.

62. O Lord God! let the haven be cast down by the fury of the storm! Let the foam of the grape tincture my soul with Thy light!

63. Bacchus grew old, and was Silenus; Pan was ever Pan for ever and ever more throughout the æons.

64. Intoxicate the inmost, O my lover, not the outermost!

65. So it was—ever the same! I have aimed at the peeled wand of my God, and I have hit; yea, I have hit.

II

1. I passed into the mountain of lapis lazuli, even as a green hawk between the pillars of turquoise that is seated upon the throne of the East.

2. So came I to Duant, the starry abode, and I heard voices crying aloud.

3. O Thou that sittest upon the Earth! (so spake a certain Veiled One to me) thou art not greater than thy mother! Thou speck of dust infinitesimal! Thou art the Lord of Glory, and the unclean dog.

4. Stooping down, dipping my wings, I came unto the darkly-splendid abodes. There in that formless abyss was I made a partaker of the Mysteries Averse.

5. I suffered the deadly embrace of the Snake and of the Goat; I paid the infernal homage to the shame of Khem.

6. Therein was this virtue, that the One became the all.

7. Moreover I beheld a vision of a river. There was a little boat thereon; and in it under purple sails was a golden woman, an image of Asi wrought in finest gold. Also the river was of blood, and the boat of shining steel. Then I loved her; and, loosing my girdle, cast myself into the stream.

8. I gathered myself into the little boat, and for many days and nights did I love her, burning beautiful incense before her.

9. Yea! I gave her of the flower of my youth.

10. But she stirred not; only by my kisses I defiled her so that she turned to blackness before me.

11. Yet I worshipped her, and gave her of the flower of my youth.

12. Also it came to pass, that thereby she sickened and corrupted before me. Almost I cast myself into the stream.

13. Then at the end appointed her body was whiter than the milk of the stars, and her lips red and warm as the sunset, and her life of a white heat like the heat of the midmost sun.

14. Then rose she up from the abyss of Ages of Sleep, and her body embraced me. Altogether I melted into her beauty and was glad.

15. The river also became the river of Amrit, and the little boat was the chariot of the flesh, and the sails thereof the blood of the heart that beareth me, that beareth me.

16. O serpent woman of the stars! I, even I, have fashioned Thee from a pale image of fine gold.

17. Also the Holy One came upon me, and I beheld a white swan floating in the blue.

18. Between its wings I sate, and the æons fled away.

19. Then the swan flew and dived and soared, yet no whither we went.

20. A little crazy boy that rode with me spake unto the swan, and said:

21. Who art thou that dost float and fly and dive and soar in the inane? Behold, these many æons have passed; whence camest thou? Whither wilt thou go?

22. And laughing I chid him, saying: No whence! No whither!

23. The swan being silent, he answered: Then, if with no goal, why this eternal journey?

24. And I laid my head against the Head of the Swan, and laughed, saying: Is there not joy ineffable in this aimless winging? Is there not weariness and impatience for who would attain to some goal?

25. And the swan was ever silent. Ah! but we floated in the infinite Abyss. Joy! Joy! White swan, bear thou ever me up between thy wings!

26. O silence! O rapture! O end of things visible and invisible! This is all mine, who am Not.

27. Radiant God! Let me fashion an image of gems and gold for Thee! that the people may cast it down and trample it to dust! That Thy glory may be seen of them.

28. Nor shall it be spoken in the markets that I am come who should come; but Thy coming shall be the one word.

29. Thou shalt manifest Thyself in the unmanifest; in the secret places men shall meet with thee, and Thou shalt overcome them.

30. I saw a pale sad boy that lay upon the marble in the sunlight, and wept. By his side was the forgotten lute. Ah! but he wept.

31. Then came an eagle from the abyss of glory and overshadowed him. So black was the shadow that he was no more visible.

32. But I heard the lute lively discoursing through the blue still air.

33. Ah! messenger of the beloved One, let Thy shadow be over me!

34. Thy name is Death, it may be, or Shame, or Love. So thou bringest me tidings of the Beloved One, I shall not ask thy name.

35. Where now is the Master? cry the little crazy boys. He is dead! He is shamed! He is wedded! and their mockery shall ring around the world.

36. But the Master shall have his reward. The laughter of the mockers shall be a ripple in the hair of the Beloved One.

37. Behold! the Abyss of the Great Deep. Therein is a mighty dolphin, lashing his sides with the force of the waves.

38. There is also an harper of gold, playing infinite tunes.

39. Then the dolphin delighted therein, and put off his body, and became a bird.

40. The harper also laid aside his harp, and played infinite tunes upon the Pan-pipe.

41. Then the bird desired exceedingly this bliss, and laying down its wings became a faun of the forest.

42. The harper also laid down his Pan-pipe, and with the human voice sang his infinite tunes.

43. Then the faun was enraptured, and followed far; at last the harper was silent, and the faun became Pan in the midst of the primal forest of Eternity.

44. Thou canst not charm the dolphin with silence, O my prophet!

45. Then the adept was rapt away in bliss, and the beyond of bliss, and exceeded the excess of excess.

46. Also his body shook and staggered with the burden of that bliss and that excess and that ultimate nameless.

47. They cried He is drunk or He is mad or He is in pain or He is about to die; and he heard them not.

48. O my Lord, my beloved! How shall I indite songs, when even the memory of the shadow of thy glory is a thing beyond all music of speech or of silence.

49. Behold! I am a man. Even a little child might not endure thee. And lo!

50. I was alone in a great park, and by a certain hillock was a ring of deep enamelled grass wherein green-clad ones, most beautiful, played.

51. In their play I came even unto the land of Fairy Sleep.

52. All night they danced and sang; but Thou art the morning, O my darling, my serpent that twinest Thee about this heart.

53. I am the heart, and Thou the serpent. Wind Thy coils closer about me, so that no light nor bliss may penetrate.

54. Crush out the blood of me, as a grape upon the tongue of a white Doric girl that languishes with her lover in the moonlight.

55. Then let the End awake. Long hast thou slept, O great God Terminus! Long ages hast thou waited at the end of the city and the roads thereof. Awake Thou! wait no more!

56. Nay, Lord! but I am come to Thee. It is I that wait at last.

57. The prophet cried against the mountain; come thou hither, that I may speak with thee!

58. The mountain stirred not. Therefore went the prophet unto the mountain, and spake unto it. But the feet of the prophet were weary, and the mountain heard not his voice.

59. But I have called unto Thee, and I have journeyed unto Thee, and it availed me not.

60. I waited patiently, and Thou wast with me from the beginning.

61. This now I know, O my beloved, and we are stretched at our ease among the vines.

62. But these thy prophets; they must cry aloud and scourge themselves; they must cross trackless wastes and unfathomed oceans; to await Thee is the end, not the beginning.

63. Let darkness cover up the writing! Let the scribe depart among his ways.

64. But thou and I are stretched at our ease among the vines; what is he?

65. O Thou beloved One! is there not an end? Nay, but there is an end. Awake! arise! gird up thy limbs, O thou runner; bear thou the Word unto the mighty cities, yea, unto the mighty cities.

III

1. Verily and Amen! I passed through the deep sea, and by the rivers of running water that abound therein, and I came unto the Land of No Desire.

2. Wherein was a white unicorn with a silver collar, whereon was graven the aphorism Linea viridis gyrat universa.

3. Then the word of Adonai came unto me by the mouth of the Magister mine, saying: O heart that art girt about with the coils of the old serpent, lift up thyself unto the mountain of initiation.

4. But I remembered. Yea, Than, yea, Theli, yea, Lilith! these three were about me from of old. For they are one.

5. Beautiful wast thou, O Lilith, thou serpent-woman!

6. Thou wast lithe and delicious to the taste, and thy perfume was of musk mingled with ambergris.

7. Close did thou cling with thy coils unto the heart, and it was as the joy of all the spring.

8. But I beheld in thee a certain taint, even in that wherein I delighted.

9. I beheld in thee the taint of thy father the ape, of thy grandsire the Blind Worm of Slime.

10. I gazed upon the Crystal of the Future, and I saw the horror of the End of thee.

11. Further, I destroyed the Time Past, and the time to Come—had I not the Power of the Sand-glass?

12. But in the very hour I beheld corruption.

13. Then I said: O my beloved, O Lord Adonai, I pray thee to loosen the coils of the serpent!

14. But she was closed fast upon me, so that my Force was stayed in its inception.

15. Also I prayed unto the Elephant God, the Lord of Beginnings, who breaketh down obstructions.

16. These gods came right quickly to mine aid. I beheld them; I joined myself unto them; I was lost in their vastness.

17. Then I beheld myself compassed about with the Infinite Circle of Emerald that encloseth the Universe.

18. O Snake of Emerald, thou hast no time Past, no time To Come. Verily Thou art not.

19. Thou art delicious beyond all taste and touch, Thou art not-to-be-beheld for glory, Thy voice is beyond the Speech and the Silence and the Speech therein, and Thy perfume is of pure ambergris, that is not weighed against the finest gold of the fine gold.

20. Also Thy coils are of infinite range; the Heart that Thou dost encircle is an Universal Heart.

21. I, and Me, and Mine were sitting with lutes in the market-place of the great city, the city of the violets and the roses.

22. The night fell, and the music of the lutes was stilled.

23. The tempest arose, and the music of the lutes was stilled.

24. The hour passed, and the music of the lutes was stilled.

25. But Thou art Eternity and Space; Thou art Matter and Motion; and Thou art the negation of all these things.

26. For there is no Symbol of Thee.

27. If I say, Come up upon the mountains! the celestial waters flow at my word. But thou art the Water beyond the waters.

28. The red three-angled heart hath been set up in Thy shrine; for the priests despised equally the shrine and the god.

29. Yet all the while Thou wast hidden therein, as the Lord of Silence is hidden in the buds of the lotus.

30. Thou art Sebek the crocodile against Asar; thou art Mati, the Slayer in the Deep. Thou art Typhon, the Wrath of the Elements, O Thou who transcendest the Forces in their Concourse and Cohesion, in their Death and their Disruption. Thou art Python, the terrible serpent about the end of all things!

31. I turned about me thrice in every way; and always I came at the last unto Thee.

32. Many things I beheld mediate and immediate; but, beholding them no more, I beheld Thee.

33. Come thou, O beloved One, O Lord God of the Universe, O Vast One, O Minute One! I am Thy beloved.

34. All day I sing of Thy delight; all night I delight in Thy song.

35. There is no other day or night than this.

36. Thou art beyond the day and the night; I am Thyself, O my Maker, my Master, my Mate!

37. I am like the little red dog that sitteth upon the knees of the Unknown.

38. Thou hast brought me into great delight. Thou hast given me of Thy flesh to eat and of Thy blood for an offering of intoxication.

39. Thou hast fastened the fangs of Eternity in my soul, and the Poison of the Infinite hath consumed me utterly.

40. I am become like a luscious devil of Italy; a fair strong woman with worn cheeks, eaten out with hunger for kisses. She hath played the harlot in divers places; she hath given her body to the beasts.

41. She hath slain her kinsfolk with strong venom of toads; she hath been scourged with many rods.

42. She hath been broken in pieces upon the Wheel; the hands of the hangman have bound her unto it.

43. The fountains of water have been loosed upon her; she hath struggled with exceeding torment.

44. She hath burst in sunder with the weight of the waters; she hath sunk into the awful Sea.

45. So am I, O Adonai, my lord, and such are the waters of Thine intolerable Essence.

46. So am I, O Adonai, my beloved, and Thou hast burst me utterly in sunder.

47. I am shed out like spilt blood upon the mountains; the Ravens of Dispersion have borne me utterly away.

48. Therefore is the seal unloosed, that guarded the Eighth Abyss; therefore is the vast sea as a veil; therefore is there a rending asunder of all things.

49. Yea, also verily Thou art the cool still water of the wizard fount. I have bathed in Thee, and lost me in Thy stillness.

50. That which went in as a brave boy of beautiful limbs cometh forth as a maiden, as a little child for perfection.

51. O Thou light and delight, ravish me away into the milky ocean of the stars!

52. O Thou Son of a light-transcending mother, blessed be Thy name, and the Name of Thy Name, throughout the ages!

53. Behold! I am a butterfly at the Source of Creation; let me die before the hour, falling dead into Thine infinite stream!

54. Also the stream of the stars floweth ever majestical unto the Abode; bear me away upon the Bosom of Nuit!

55. This is the world of the waters of Maim; this is the bitter water that becometh sweet. Thou art beautiful and bitter, O golden one, O my Lord Adonai, O thou Abyss of Sapphire!

56. I follow Thee, and the waters of Death fight strenuously against me. I pass into the Waters beyond Death and beyond Life.

57. How shall I answer the foolish man? In no way shall he come to the Identity of Thee!

58. But I am the Fool that heedeth not the Play of the Magician. Me doth the Woman of the Mysteries instruct in vain; I have burst the bonds of Love and of Power and of Worship.

59. Therefore is the Eagle made one with the man, and the gallows of infamy dance with the fruit of the just.

60. I have descended, O my darling, into the black shining waters, and I have plucked Thee forth as a black pearl of infinite preciousness.

61. I have gone down, O my God, into the abyss of the all, and I have found Thee in the midst under the guise of No Thing.

62. But as Thou art the Last, Thou art also the Next, and as the Next do I reveal Thee to the multitude.

63. They that ever desired Thee shall obtain Thee, even at the End of their Desire.

64. Glorious, glorious, glorious art Thou, O my lover supernal, O Self of myself.

65. For I have found Thee alike in the Me and the Thee; there is no difference, O my beautiful, my desirable One! In the One and the Many have I found Thee; yea, I have found Thee.

IV

1. O crystal heart! I the Serpent clasp Thee; I drive home mine head into the central core of Thee, O God my beloved.

2. Even as on the resounding wind-swept heights of Mitylene some god-like woman casts aside the lyre, and with her locks aflame as an aureole, plunges into the wet heart of the creation, so I, O Lord my God!

3. There is a beauty unspeakable in the heart of corruption, where the flowers are aflame.

4. Ah me! but the thirst of Thy joy parches up this throat, so that I cannot sing.

5. I will make a little boat of my tongue, and explore the unknown rivers. It may be that the everlasting salt may turn to sweetness, and that my life may be no longer athirst.

6. O ye that drink of the brine of your desire, ye are nigh to madness! Your torture increaseth as ye drink, yet still ye drink. Come up through the creeks to the fresh water; I shall be waiting for you with my kisses.

7. As the bezoar-stone that is found in the belly of the cow, so is my lover among lovers.

8. O honey boy! Bring me Thy cool limbs hither! Let us sit awhile in the orchard, until the sun go down! Let us feast on the cool grass! Bring wine, ye slaves, that the cheeks of my boy may flush red.

9. In the garden of immortal kisses, O thou brilliant One, shine forth! Make Thy mouth an opium-poppy, that one kiss is the key to the infinite sleep and lucid, the sleep of Shi-loh-am.

10. In my sleep I beheld the Universe like a clear crystal without one speck.

11. There are purse-proud penniless ones that stand at the door of the tavern and prate of their feats of wine-bibbing.

12. There are purse-proud penniless ones that stand at the door of the tavern and revile the guests.

13. The guests dally upon couches of mother-of-pearl in the garden; the noise of the foolish men is hidden from them.

14. Only the inn-keeper feareth lest the favour of the king be withdrawn from him.

15. Thus spake the Magister V.V.V.V.V. unto Adonai his god, as they played together in the starlight over against the deep black pool that is in the Holy Place of the Holy House beneath the Altar of the Holiest One.

16. But Adonai laughed, and played more languidly.

17. Then the scribe took note, and was glad. But Adonai had no fear of the Magician and his play. For it was Adonai who had taught all his tricks to the Magician.

18. And the Magister entered into the play of the Magician. When the Magician laughed he laughed; all as a man should do.

19. And Adonai said: Thou art enmeshed in the web of the Magician. This He said subtly, to try him.

20. But the Magister gave the sign of the Magistry, and laughed back on him: O Lord, O beloved, did these fingers relax on Thy curls, or these eyes turn away from Thine eye?

21. And Adonai delighted in him exceedingly.

22. Yea, O my master, thou art the beloved of the Beloved One; the Bennu Bird is set up in Philæ not in vain.

23. I who was the priestess of Ahathoor rejoice in your love. Arise, O Nile-God, and devour the holy place of the Cow of Heaven! Let the milk of the stars be drunk up by Sebek the dweller of Nile!

24. Arise, O serpent Apep, Thou art Adonai the beloved one! Thou art my darling and my lord, and Thy poison is sweeter than the kisses of Isis the mother of the Gods!

25. For Thou art He! Yea, Thou shalt swallow up Asi and Asar, and the children of Ptah. Thou shalt pour forth a flood of poison to destroy the works of the Magician. Only the Destroyer shall devour Thee; Thou shalt blacken his throat, wherein his spirit abideth. Ah, serpent Apep, but I love Thee!

26. My God! Let Thy secret fang pierce to the marrow of the little secret bone that I have kept against the Day of Vengeance of Hoor-Ra. Let Kheph-Ra sound his sharded drone! let the jackals of Day and Night howl in the wilderness of Time! let the towers of the Universe totter, and the guardians hasten away! For my Lord hath revealed himself as a mighty serpent, and my heart is the blood of His body.

27. I am like a love-sick courtesan of Corinth. I have toyed with kings and captains, and made them my slaves. To-day I am the slave of the little asp of death; and who shall loosen our love?

28. Weary, weary! saith the scribe, who shall lead me to the sight of the Rapture of my master?

29. The body is weary and the soul is sore weary and sleep weighs down their eyelids; yet ever abides the sure consciousness of ecstasy,

unknown, yet known in that its being is certain. O Lord, be my helper, and bring me to the bliss of the Beloved!

30. I came to the house of the Beloved, and the wine was like fire that flieth with green wings through the world of the waters.

31. I felt the red lips of nature and the black lips of perfection. Like sisters they fondled me their little brother; they decked me out as a bride; they mounted me for Thy bridal chamber.

32. They fled away at Thy coming; I was alone before Thee.

33. I trembled at Thy coming, O my God, for Thy messenger was more terrible than the Death-star.

34. On the threshold stood the fulminant figure of Evil, the Horror of emptiness, with his ghastly eyes like poisonous wells. He stood, and the chamber was corrupt; the air stank. He was an old and gnarled fish more hideous than the shells of Abaddon.

35. He enveloped me with his demon tentacles; yea, the eight fears took hold upon me.

36. But I was anointed with the right sweet oil of the Magister; I slipped from the embrace as a stone from the sling of a boy of the woodlands.

37. I was smooth and hard as ivory; the horror gat no hold. Then at the noise of the wind of Thy coming he was dissolved away, and the abyss of the great void was unfolded before me.

38. Across the waveless sea of eternity Thou didst ride with Thy captains and Thy hosts; with Thy chariots and horsemen and spearmen didst Thou travel through the blue.

39. Before I saw Thee Thou wast already with me; I was smitten through by Thy marvellous spear.

40. I was stricken as a bird by the bolt of the thunderer; I was pierced as the thief by the Lord of the Garden.

41. O my Lord, let us sail upon the sea of blood!

42. There is a deep taint beneath the ineffable bliss; it is the taint of generation.

43. Yea, though the flower wave bright in the sunshine, the root is deep in the darkness of earth.

44. Praise to thee, O beautiful dark earth, thou art the mother of a million myriads of myriads of flowers.

45. Also I beheld my God, and the countenance of Him was a thousandfold brighter than the lightning. Yet in his heart I beheld the slow and dark One, the ancient one, the devourer of His children.

46. In the height and the abyss, O my beautiful, there is no thing, verily, there is no thing at all, that is not altogether and perfectly fashioned for Thy delight.

47. Light cleaveth unto Light, and filth to filth; with pride one contemneth another. But not Thou, who art all, and beyond it; who art absolved from the Division of the Shadows.

48. O day of Eternity, let Thy wave break in foamless glory of sapphire upon the laborious coral of our making!

49. We have made us a ring of glistening white sand, strewn wisely in the midst of the Delightful Ocean.

50. Let the palms of brilliance flower upon our island; we shall eat of their fruit, and be glad.

51. But for me the lustral water, the great ablution, the dissolving of the soul in that resounding abyss.

52. I have a little son like a wanton goat; my daughter is like an unfledged eaglet; they shall get them fins, that they may swim.

53. That they may swim, O my beloved, swim far in the warm honey of Thy being, O blessed one, O boy of beatitude!

54. This heart of mine is girt about with the serpent that devoureth his own coils.

55. When shall there be an end, O my darling, O when shall the Universe and the Lord thereof be utterly swallowed up?

56. Nay! who shall devour the Infinite? who shall undo the Wrong of the Beginning?

57. Thou criest like a white cat upon the roof of the Universe; there is none to answer Thee.

58. Thou art like a lonely pillar in the midst of the sea; there is none to behold Thee, O Thou who beholdest all!

59. Thou dost faint, thou dost fail, thou scribe; cried the desolate Voice; but I have filled thee with a wine whose savour thou knowest not.

60. It shall avail to make drunken the people of the old gray sphere that rolls in the infinite Far-off; they shall lap the wine as dogs that lap the blood of a beautiful courtesan pierced through by the Spear of a swift rider through the city.

61. I too am the Soul of the desert; thou shalt seek me yet again in the wilderness of sand.

62. At thy right hand a great lord and a comely; at thy left hand a woman clad in gossamer and gold and having the stars in her hair. Ye shall journey far into a land of pestilence and evil; ye shall encamp in the river of a foolish city forgotten; there shall ye meet with Me.

63. There will I make Mine habitation; as for bridal will I come bedecked and anointed; there shall the Consummation be accomplished.

64. O my darling, I also wait for the brilliance of the hour ineffable, when the universe shall be like a girdle for the midst of the ray of our love, extending beyond the permitted end of the endless One.

65. Then, O thou heart, will I the serpent eat thee wholly up; yea, I will eat thee wholly up.

V

1. Ah! my Lord Adonai, that dalliest with the Magister in the Treasure-House of Pearls, let me listen to the echo of your kisses.

2. Is not the starry heaven shaken as a leaf at the tremulous rapture of your love? Am not I the flying spark of light whirled away by the great wind of your perfection?

3. Yea, cried the Holy One, and from Thy spark will I the Lord kindle a great light; I will burn through the grey city in the old and desolate land; I will cleanse it from its great impurity.

4. And thou, O prophet, shalt see these things, and thou shalt heed them not.

5. Now is the Pillar established in the Void; now is Asi fulfilled of Asar; now is Hoor let down into the Animal Soul of Things like a fiery star that falleth upon the darkness of the earth.

6. Through the midnight thou art dropt, O my child, my conqueror, my sword-girt captain, O Hoor! and they shall find thee as a black gnarled glittering stone, and they shall worship thee.

7. My prophet shall prophesy concerning thee; around thee the maidens shall dance, and bright babes be born unto them. Thou shalt inspire the proud ones with infinite pride, and the humble ones with an ecstasy of abasement; all this shall transcend the Known and the

Unknown with somewhat that hath no name. For it is as the abyss of the Arcanum that is opened in the secret Place of Silence.

8. Thou hast come hither, O my prophet, through grave paths. Thou hast eaten of the dung of the Abominable Ones; thou hast prostrated thyself before the Goat and the Crocodile; the evil men have made thee a plaything; thou hast wandered as a painted harlot, ravishing with sweet scent and Chinese colouring, in the streets; thou hast darkened thine eyepits with Kohl; thou hast tinted thy lips with vermilion; thou hast plastered thy cheeks with ivory enamels. Thou hast played the wanton in every gate and by-way of the great city. The men of the city have lusted after thee to abuse thee and to beat thee. They have mouthed the golden spangles of fine dust wherewith thou didst bedeck thine hair; they have scourged the painted flesh of thee with their whips; thou hast suffered unspeakable things.

9. But I have burnt within thee as a pure flame without oil. In the midnight I was brighter than the moon; in the daytime I exceeded utterly the sun; in the byways of thy being I flamed, and dispelled the illusion.

10. Therefore thou art wholly pure before Me; therefore thou art My virgin unto eternity.

11. Therefore I love thee with surpassing love; therefore they that despise thee shall adore thee.

12. Thou shalt be lovely and pitiful toward them; thou shalt heal them of the unutterable evil.

13. They shall change in their destruction, even as two dark stars that crash together in the abyss, and blaze up in an infinite burning.

14. All this while did Adonai pierce my being with his sword that hath four blades; the blade of the thunderbolt, the blade of the Pylon, the blade of the serpent, the blade of the Phallus.

15. Also he taught me the holy unutterable word Ararita, so that I melted the sixfold gold into a single invisible point, whereof naught may be spoken.

16. For the Magistry of this Opus is a secret magistry; and the sign of the master thereof is a certain ring of lapis-lazuli with the name of my master, who am I, and the Eye in the Midst thereof.

17. Also He spake and said: This is a secret sign, and thou shalt not disclose it unto the profane, nor unto the neophyte, nor unto the zelator, nor unto the practicus, nor unto the philosophus, nor unto the lesser adept, nor unto the greater adept.

18. But unto the exempt adept thou shalt disclose thyself if thou have need of him for the lesser operations of thine art.

19. Accept the worship of the foolish people, whom thou hatest. The Fire is not defiled by the altars of the Ghebers, nor is the Moon contaminated by the incense of them that adore the Queen of Night.

20. Thou shalt dwell among the people as a precious diamond among cloudy diamonds, and crystals, and pieces of glass. Only the eye of the just merchant shall behold thee, and plunging in his hand shall single thee out and glorify thee before men.

21. But thou shalt heed none of this. Thou shalt be ever the heart, and I the serpent will coil close about thee. My coils shall never relax throughout the æons. Neither change nor sorrow nor unsubstantiality shall have thee; for thou art passed beyond all these.

22. Even as the diamond shall glow red for the rose, and green for the rose-leaf; so shalt thou abide apart from the Impressions.

23. I am thou, and the Pillar is established in the void.

24. Also thou art beyond the stabilities of Being and of Consciousness and of Bliss; for I am thou, and the Pillar is established in the void.

25. Also thou shalt discourse of these things unto the man that writeth them, and he shall partake of them as a sacrament; for I who am thou am he, and the Pillar is established in the void.

26. From the Crown to the Abyss, so goeth it single and erect. Also the limitless sphere shall glow with the brilliance thereof.

27. Thou shalt rejoice in the pools of adorable water; thou shalt bedeck thy damsels with pearls of fecundity; thou shalt light flame like licking tongues of liquor of the Gods between the pools.

28. Also thou shalt convert the all-sweeping air into the winds of pale water, thou shalt transmute the earth into a blue abyss of wine.

29. Ruddy are the gleams of ruby and gold that sparkle therein; one drop shall intoxicate the Lord of the Gods my servant.

30. Also Adonai spake unto V.V.V.V.V. saying: O my little one, my tender one, my little amorous one, my gazelle, my beautiful, my boy, let us fill up the pillar of the Infinite with an infinite kiss!

31. So that the stable was shaken and the unstable became still.

32. They that beheld it cried with a formidable affright: The end of things is come upon us.

33. And it was even so.

34. Also I was in the spirit vision and beheld a parricidal pomp of atheists, coupled by two and by two in the supernal ecstasy of the stars. They did laugh and rejoice exceedingly, being clad in purple robes and drunken with purple wine, and their whole soul was one purple flower-flame of holiness.

35. They beheld not God; they beheld not the Image of God; therefore were they arisen to the Palace of the Splendour Ineffable. A sharp sword smote out before them, and the worm Hope writhed in its death-agony under their feet.

36. Even as their rapture shore asunder the visible Hope, so also the Fear Invisible fled away and was no more.

37. O ye that are beyond Aormuzdi and Ahrimanes! blessed are ye unto the ages.

38. They shaped Doubt as a sickle, and reaped the flowers of Faith for their garlands.

39. They shaped Ecstasy as a spear, and pierced the ancient dragon that sat upon the stagnant water.

40. Then the fresh springs were unloosed, that the folk athirst might be at ease.

41. And again I was caught up into the presence of my Lord Adonai, and the knowledge and Conversation of the Holy One, the Angel that Guardeth me.

42. O Holy Exalted One, O Self beyond self, O Self-Luminous Image of the Unimaginable Naught, O my darling, my beautiful, come Thou forth and follow me.

43. Adonai, divine Adonai, let Adonai initiate refulgent dalliance! Thus I concealed the name of Her name that inspireth my rapture, the scent of whose body bewildereth the soul, the light of whose soul abaseth this body unto the beasts.

44. I have sucked out the blood with my lips; I have drained Her beauty of its sustenance; I have abased Her before me, I have mastered Her, I have possessed Her, and Her life is within me. In Her blood I inscribe the secret riddles of the Sphinx of the Gods, that none shall understand,—save only the pure and voluptuous, the chaste and obscene, the androgyne and gynander that have passed beyond the bars of the prison that the old Slime of Khem set up in the Gates of Amennti.

45. O my adorable, my delicious one, all night will I pour out the libation on Thine altars; all night will I burn the sacrifice of blood; all

night will I swing the thurible of my delight before Thee, and the fervour of the orisons shall intoxicate Thy nostrils.

46. O Thou who camest from the land of the Elephant, girt about with the tiger's pell, and garlanded with the lotus of the spirit, do Thou inebriate my life with Thy madness, that She leap at my passing.

47. Bid thy maidens who follow Thee bestrew us a bed of flowers immortal, that we may take our pleasure thereupon. Bid Thy satyrs heap thorns among the flowers, that we may take our pain thereon. Let the pleasure and pain be mingled in one supreme offering unto the Lord Adonai!

48. Also I heard the voice of Adonai the Lord the desirable one concerning that which is beyond.

49. Let not the dwellers in Thebai and the temples thereof prate ever of the Pillars of Hercules and the Ocean of the West. Is not the Nile a beautiful water?

50. Let not the priest of Isis uncover the nakedness of Nuit, for every step is a death and a birth. The priest of Isis lifted the veil of Isis, and was slain by the kisses of her mouth. Then was he the priest of Nuit, and drank of the milk of the stars.

51. Let not the failure and the pain turn aside the worshippers. The foundations of the pyramid were hewn in the living rock ere sunset; did the king weep at dawn that the crown of the pyramid was yet unquarried in the distant land?

52. There was also an humming-bird that spake unto the horned cerastes, and prayed him for poison. And the great snake of Khem the Holy One, the royal Uræus serpent, answered him and said:

53. I sailed over the sky of Nu in the car called Millions-of-Years, and I saw not any creature upon Seb that was equal to me. The venom of my fang is the inheritance of my father, and of my father's father; and how shall I give it unto thee? Live thou and thy children as I and my

fathers have lived, even unto an hundred millions of generations, and it may be that the mercy of the Mighty Ones may bestow upon thy children a drop of the poison of eld.

54. Then the humming-bird was afflicted in his spirit, and he flew unto the flowers, and it was as if naught had been spoken between them. Yet in a little while a serpent struck him that he died.

55. But an Ibis that meditated upon the bank of Nile the beautiful god listened and heard. And he laid aside his Ibis ways, and became as a serpent, saying Peradventure in an hundred millions of millions of generations of my children, they shall attain to a drop of the poison of the fang of the Exalted One.

56. And behold! ere the moon waxed thrice he became an Uræus serpent, and the poison of the fang was established in him and his seed even for ever and for ever.

57. O thou Serpent Apep, my Lord Adonai, it is a speck of minutest time, this travelling through eternity, and in Thy sight the landmarks are of fair white marble untouched by the tool of the graver. Therefore Thou art mine, even now and for ever and for everlasting. Amen.

58. Moreover, I heard the voice of Adonai: Seal up the book of the Heart and the Serpent; in the number five and sixty seal thou the holy book. As fine gold that is beaten into a diadem for the fair queen of Pharaoh, as great stones that are cemented together into the Pyramid of the ceremony of the Death of Asar, so do thou bind together the words and the deeds, so that in all is one Thought of Me thy delight Adonai.

59. And I answered and said: It is done even according unto Thy word. And it was done. And they that read the book and debated thereon passed into the desolate Land of Barren Words. And they that sealed up the book into their blood were the chosen of Adonai, and the Thought of Adonai was a Word and a Deed; and they abode in the Land that the far-off travellers call Naught.

60. O land beyond honey and spice and all perfection! I will dwell therein with my Lord for ever.

61. And the Lord Adonai delighteth in me, and I bear the Cup of his gladness unto the weary ones of the old grey land.

62. They that drink thereof are smitten of disease; the abomination hath hold upon them, and their torment is like the thick black smoke of the evil abode.

63. But the chosen ones drank thereof, and became even as my Lord, my beautiful, my desirable one. There is no wine like unto this wine.

64. They are gathered together into a glowing heart, as Ra that gathereth his clouds about Him at eventide into a molten sea of joy; and the snake that is the crown of Ra bindeth them about with the golden girdle of the death-kisses.

65. So also is the end of the book, and the Lord Adonai is about it on all sides like a Thunderbolt, and a Pylon, and a Snake, and a Phallus, and in the midst thereof He is like the Woman that jetteth out the milk of the stars from her paps; yea, the milk of the stars from her paps.

COLOPHON

This compilation of the Libri of the Probationer grade has been prepared by Saklas Publishing as a service to aspirants of the A∴A∴ and students of the Western Mystery Tradition. The texts herein are drawn from the Class A, B, D, and E publications of the A∴A∴ as originally published in The Equinox and related sources.

These texts are in the public domain. This compilation does not claim copyright over the original works, which belong to the corpus of Thelemic Holy Books and instructional literature. The arrangement and introductory material are offered freely for the benefit of all seekers.

"The Method of Science—The Aim of Religion"

Saklas Publishing

Assembled by

Frater Lachesis Peyton

Tat Tvam Asi

MMXXVI

www.ingramcontent.com/pod-product-compliance
Lightning Source LLC
Chambersburg PA
CBHW021206130626
46554CB00005B/2008